CAMBRIDGE LIBRARY COLLECTION

Books of enduring scholarly value

Printing and Publishing History

The interface between authors and their readers is a fascinating subject in its own right, revealing a great deal about social attitudes, technological progress, aesthetic values, fashionable interests, political positions, economic constraints, and individual personalities. This part of the Cambridge Library Collection reissues classic studies in the area of printing and publishing history that shed light on developments in typography and book design, printing and binding, the rise and fall of publishing houses and periodicals, and the roles of authors and illustrators. It documents the ebb and flow of the book trade supplying a wide range of customers with products from almanacs to novels, bibles to erotica, and poetry to statistics.

How to Make an Index

Henry Benjamin Wheatley (1838–1917) was a bibliographer and editor with a prodigious output of books and articles to his name. Brought up after the death of both his parents by his brother Benjamin Robert, himself a skilled bibliographer and cataloguer, Henry compiled catalogues for learned societies and worked for many years for the Royal Society and the Royal Society of Arts; he was a founder member of the Library Association and of the Early English Text Society, and produced an edition of Pepys' diary which was not superseded until the 1970s. This work is one of two which he produced on the subject of indexing, and which led him to become known as 'the father of British indexing': the Wheatley Medal awarded by the Society of Indexers is named after him. This book, published in 1902, sets out the rules and practicalities of indexing, and also contains examples of how *not* to make an index; it was for many years the text to which all professional indexers referred, and still makes fascinating reading today.

T0370719

How to
Make an Index

HENRY BENJAMIN WHEATLEY

CAMBRIDGE UNIVERSITY PRESS

Cambridge, New York, Melbourne, Madrid, Cape Town, Singapore,
São Paolo, Delhi, Dubai, Tokyo, Mexico City

Published in the United States of America by Cambridge University Press, New York

www.cambridge.org
Information on this title: www.cambridge.org/9781108021500

This edition first published 1902
This digitally printed version 2010

ISBN 978-1-108-02150-0 Paperback

The Book-Lover's Library.

Edited by

Henry B. Wheatley, F.S.A

HOW TO MAKE AN INDEX

BY

HENRY B. WHEATLEY, F.S.A.

AUTHOR OF " HOW TO CATALOGUE A LIBRARY "
" HOW TO FORM A LIBRARY," ETC., ETC.

"M. Bochart . . . me prioit surtout d'y faire un
Index, etant, disoit-il, l'âme des gros livres."—
Menagiana.

LONDON

ELLIOT STOCK, 62, PATERNOSTER ROW

1902

PREFACE.

I<small>N</small> 1878 *I wrote for the Index Society, as its first publication, a pamphlet entitled " What is an Index ? " The present little book is compiled on somewhat similar lines ; but, as its title suggests, it is drawn up with a more practical object. The first four chapters are " Historical," and the other four are " Practical" ; but the historical portion is intended to lead up to the practical portion by showing what to imitate and what to avoid.*

There has been of late years a considerable change in public opinion with respect to the difficulties attending the making of both indexes and catalogues. It was once a common opinion that anyone without preparatory knowledge or experience could make an index. That that opinion is not true is amply proved, I hope, in the chapter on the " Bad Indexer."

I have attempted to describe the best way of setting to work on an index. To do this with any hope of success it is necessary to give details that may to some seem puerile, but I have ventured on particulars for which I hope I may not be condemned.

I must also ask the forbearance of my readers for the constant use of the personal pronoun. If I could have left it out, I would gladly have done so ; but to a great extent this book relates to the experiences of an old indexer. They must be taken for what they are worth, and I hope forgiveness will be extended to me for the form in which these experiences are related.

H. B. W.

CONTENTS.

HISTORICAL.

CHAPTER III.

THE BAD INDEXER.

CHAPTER IV.

THE GOOD INDEXER.

PRACTICAL.

CHAPTER V.

DIFFERENT CLASSES OF INDEXES.

CHAPTER VI.

GENERAL RULES FOR ALPHABETICAL INDEXES.

CHAPTER VII.

HOW TO SET ABOUT AN INDEX.

CHAPTER VIII.

GENERAL OR UNIVERSAL INDEX.

HOW TO MAKE AN INDEX.

CHAPTER I.

INTRODUCTION.

"I for my part venerate the inventor of
Indexes; and I know not to whom to yield the
preference, either to Hippocrates, who was the
great anatomiser of the human body, or to that
unknown labourer in literature who first laid
open the nerves and arteries of a book."
—ISAAC DISRAELI, *Literary Miscellanies.*

T is generally agreed that that
only is true knowledge which
consists of information assimi-
lated by our own minds. Mere
disjointed facts kept in our memories have
no right to be described as knowledge. It

is this understanding that has made many
writers jeer at so-called index-learning.
Thus, in the seventeenth century, Joseph
Glanville, writing in his *Vanity of Dogma-
tizing*, says : " Methinks 'tis a pitiful piece
of knowledge that can be learnt from an
index, and a poor ambition to be rich
in the inventory of another's treasure."
Dr. Watts alluded to those whose "learning reaches no farther than the tables of
contents "; but then he added a sentence
which quite takes the sting from what
he had said before, and shows how
absolutely needful an index is.   He says :
" If a book has no index or table of
contents, 'tis very useful to make one as
you are reading it."

Swift had his say on index-learning, too.
In the *Tale of a Tub* (Section VII.) he
wrote :   " The most accomplisht way of
using books at present is twofold : Either
serve them as some men do Lords, learn
their titles exactly, and then brag of their
acquaintance.   Or secondly, which indeed is the choicer, the profounder and
politer method, to get a thorough insight
into the Index, by which the whole book

is governed and turned, like fishes by the tail. For to enter the palace of Learning at the great gate, requires an expense of time and forms; therefore men of much haste and little ceremony are content to get in by the back-door. For, the Arts are all in a flying march, and therefore more easily subdued by attacking them in the rear. . . . Thus men catch Knowledge by throwing their wit on the posteriors of a book, as boys do sparrows with flinging salt upon their tails. Thus human life is best understood by the wise man's Rule of regarding the end. Thus are the Sciences found like Hercules' oxen, by tracing them backwards. Thus are old Sciences unravelled like old stockings, by beginning at the foot."

Thomas Fuller, with his usual common-sense, wisely argues that the diligent man should not be deprived of a tool because the idler may misuse it. He writes: "An Index is a necessary implement and no impediment of a book except in the same sense wherein the carriages [*i.e.* things carried] of an army

are termed *impedimenta.* Without this a
large author is but a labyrinth without
a clue to direct the reader therein. I
confess there is a lazy kind of learning
which is only indical, when scholars (like
adders which only bite the horses' heels)
nibble but at the tables, which are calces
librorum, neglecting the body of the
book. But though the idle deserve no
crutches (let not a staff be used by them
but on them), pity it is the weary should
be denied the benefit thereof, and
industrious scholars prohibited the accommodation of an index, most used by
those who most pretend to contemn it."

The same objection to "indical" learning is urged to-day, but it is really a futile
one. No man can know everything ; he
may possess much true knowledge, but
there is a mass of matter that the learned
man knows he can never master completely. He does not care to burden
his mind with what might be to him
useless lumber. In this case his object
is only to know where he can find the
information when he wants it. Indexes
are of the greatest help to these men,

and for their purposes the indexes ought
to be well made. But it is needless to
labour this point, for has not Johnson, in
his clear and virile language, said the last
word on the matter ?—" Knowledge is of
two kinds; we know a subject ourselves,
or we know where we can find information
upon it. When we inquire into any
subject, the first thing we have to do is
to know what books have treated of it.
This leads us to look at catalogues and
the backs of books."

Before going further, it would be well
for author and reader to come to an
agreement as to what an index really is.
An index may, in certain circumstances,
be arranged in the order of the book,
like a table of contents, or it may be
classified or chronological; but the index
to a book such as we all think of when we
speak of an index should be alphabetical.
The other arrangements must be exceptional, because the books indexed are
exceptional.

It is strange, however, to find how
long the world was in coming to this
very natural conclusion. The first attempt

at indexing a book was in the form of an
abstract of contents in the order of the
book itself. Seneca, in sending certain
volumes to his friend Lucilius, accom-
panied them with notes of particular
passages, so that he "who only aimed
at the useful might be spared the trouble
of examining them entire." Cicero used
the word "index" to express the table
of contents of a book, and he asked his
friend Atticus to send him two library
clerks to repair his books. He added
that he wished them to bring with them
some parchment to make indexes upon.

Many old manuscripts have useful
tables of contents, and in Dan Michel's
Ayenbite of Inwyt (1340) there is a very
full table with the heading : " Thise
byeth the capiteles of the boc volȝinde."

It was only a step to arrange this table
of contents in the order of the alphabet,
and thus form a true index ; but it took a
long time to take this step. Alphabetical
indexes of names are to be found in some
old manuscript books, but it may be said
that the general use of the alphabetical
arrangement is one of those labour-

saving expedients which came into use
with the invention of printing.

Erasmus supplied alphabetical indexes
to many of his books; but even in his
time arrangement in alphabetical order
was by no means considered indispensable
in an index, and the practice came into
general use very slowly.

The word "index" had a hard fight
with such synonyms as "calendar," "catalogue," "inventory," "register," "summary," "syllabus." In time it beat all
its companions in the race, although it
had the longest struggle with the word
"table." *

* All these words are fairly common; but there
is another which was used only occasionally in the
sixteenth century. This is "pye," supposed to be
derived from the Greek Πίναξ, among the mean-
ings of which, as given in Liddell and Scott's
Lexicon, is, "A register, or list." The late Sir
T. Duffus Hardy, in some observations on the
derivation of the word "Pye-Book," remarks that
the earliest use he had noted of pye in this sense
is dated 1547 : "A Pye of all the names of such
Balives as been to accompte pro anno regni regis
Edwardi Sexti primo."—*Appendix to the "35th
Report of the Deputy Keeper of the Public
Records,"* p. 195.

Cicero used the word "index," and explained it by the word "syllabus." Index was not generally acknowledged as an English word until late in the seventeenth century.

North's racy translation of Plutarch's *Lives*, the book so diligently used by Shakespeare in the production of his Roman histories, contains an alphabetical index at the end, but it is called a table. On the title-page of Baret's *Alvearie* (1573), one of the early English dictionaries, mention is made of "two *Tables* in the ende of this booke"; but the tables themselves, which were compiled by Abraham Fleming, being lists of the Latin and French words, are headed 'Index." Between these two tables, in the edition of 1580, is "an Abecedarie, Index or Table" of Proverbs. The word "index" is not included in the body of the dictionary, where, however, "Table" and "Regester" are inserted. "Table" is defined as "a booke or regester for memorie of thinges," and "regester" as "a reckeninge booke wherein thinges dayly done be written." By this it is

clear that Baret did not consider index
to be an English word.

At the end of Johnson's edition of
Gerarde's *Herbal* (1636) is an "Index
Latinus," followed by a "Table of
English names," although a few years
previously Minsheu had given "index"
a sort of half-hearted welcome into his
dictionary. Under that word in the
Guide into Tongues (1617) is the entry,
"vide Table in Booke, in litera T.,"
where we read, "a Table in a booke
or Index." Even when acknowledged
as an English word, it was frequently
differentiated from the analytical table :
for instance, Dugdale's *Warwickshire*
contains an "Index of Towns and
Places," and a "Table of men's names
and matters of most note "; and Scobell's
Acts and Ordinances of Parliament
(1640–1656), published 1658, has "An
Alphabetical Table of the most material
contents of the whole book," preceded
by "An Index of the general titles
comprized in the ensuing Table." There
are a few exceptions to the rule here
set forth : for instance, Plinie's *Natural*

Historie of the World, translated by
Philemon Holland (1601), has at the
beginning, "The Inventorie or Index
containing the contents of 37 bookes,"
and at the end, " An Index pointing to the
principal matters." In Speed's *History
of Great Britaine* (1611) there is an
" Index or Alphabetical Table containing
the principal matters in this history."

The introduction of the word " index "
into English from the Latin word in the
nominative shows that it dates from a
comparatively recent period, and came
into the language through literature and
not through speech. In earlier times it
was the custom to derive our words from
the Latin accusative. The Italian word
indice was from the accusative, and this
word was used by Ben Jonson when he
wrote, "too much talking is ever the
indice of a fool " (*Discoveries*, ed. 1640,
p. 93). The French word *indice* has a
different meaning from the Italian *indice*,
and according to Littré is not derived
from *index*, but from *indicium*. It is
possible that Jonson's "indice" is the
French, and not the Italian, word.

Drayton uses "index" as an indicator :
"Lest when my lisping guiltie tongue should hault,
My lookes might prove the index to my fault."
—*Rosamond's Epistle*, lines 103-104.

Shakespeare uses the word as a table
of contents at the beginning of a book
rather than as an alphabetical list at the
end : for instance, Nestor says :

" Our imputation shall be oddly poised
In this wild action : for the success,
Although particular, shall give a scantling
Of good or bad unto the general ;
And in such *indexes*, although small pricks
To their *subsequent volumes*, there is seen
The baby figure of the giant mass
Of things to come at large."
—*Troilus and Cressida*, I. 3.

Buckingham threatens :
" I'll sort occasion,
As *index* to the story we late talk'd of,
To part the queen's proud kindred from the king."
—*Richard III.*, II. 2.

And Iago refers to " an *index* and ob-
scure prologue to the history of lust and
foul thoughts " (*Othello*, II. 1). It may be
remarked in the quotation from *Troilus
and Cressida* that Shakespeare uses the
proper plural—" indexes "—instead of

"indices," which even now some writers
insist on using. No word can be considered as thoroughly naturalised that is
allowed to take the plural form of the
language from which it is obtained. The
same remark applies to the word
"appendix," the plural of which some
write as "appendices" instead of
"appendixes." In the case of "indices,"
this word is correctly appropriated to
another use.

Indexes need not necessarily be dry;
and some of the old ones are full of
quaint touches which make them by no
means the least interesting portion of the
books they adorn. John Florio's translation of Montaigne's *Essays* contains "An
Index or Table directing to many of the
principal matters and personages mentioned in this Booke," which is full of
curious entries and odd cross references.
The entries are not in perfect alphabetical
order. A few of the headings will give a
good idea of the whole :

"Action better than speach."
"Action to some is rest."
"Beasts are Physitians, Logitians,

Musitians, Artists, Students, Politikes, Docible, Capable of Military Order, of Affections, of Justice, of Friendship, of Husbandry, of thankefulnesse and of compassion," etc.

" Bookes and Bookishnesse."

" Bookes not so profitable as Conference —as deare as children."

" Bruit creatures have imagination."

" Cloysters not without cares."

" Good fortune not to be despised altogether."

" Societie of bookes."

Here are some of the cross references :

" Alteration *vide* Inconstancy."

" Amitie *vide* Friendship."

" Ant *vide* Emmets."

" Apprehension *vide* Imagination."

" Balladmakers *vide* Rymers."

" Boasting *vide* Vaunting."

" Chance *vide* Fortune."

" Common People *vide* the Vulgar."

" Disparity *vide* Equality."

" Emperickes *vide* Physitians."

An instance of how loosely the word "index" has been used will be found in Robert Boyle's *Some Considerations touching*

*the Usefulnesse of Experimental Natural
Philosophy* (Oxford, 1663). This book
is divided into two parts, and at the end
of each part is "The Index." This so-
called index is arranged in order of the
pages, and is really only a full table of
contents.

Indexes did not become at all common
till the sixteenth century, and Mr.
Cornelius Walford asked in *Notes and
Queries* what was the earliest index. Mr.
Edward Solly answered : "Polydore Vergil
in *Anglicæ Historiæ* (1556), has what may
fairly be called a good index—thirty-seven
pages. This may be taken as a starting-
point as to date ; and we may ask for
earlier examples" (6th S. xi. 155). Another
contributor referred to an earlier edition of
Polydore Vergil (1546), and still another
one cited Lyndewood's *Provinciale* (1525),
which has several indexes.

One old index may be singled out as
having caused its author serious misfortune. William Prynne concocted a
most wonderful attack upon the "stage"
under the title of *Histrio-Mastix* (1633),
which is absolutely unreadable by reason

of the vast mass of authorities gathered from every century and every nation, to prove the wickedness of play-acting. Carlyle refers to the *Histrio-Mastix* as "a book still extant, but never more to be read by mortal."

If Prynne had sent his child out into the world without an index, he might have escaped from persecution, as no one would have found out the enormities which were supposed to lurk within the pages of the book. But he was unwise enough to add a most elaborate index, in which all the attacks upon a calling that received the sanction of the Court were arranged in a convenient form for reference. Attorney-General Noy found that the author himself had forged the weapons which he (the prosecutor) could use in the attack. This is proved by a passage in Noy's speech at Prynne's trial, where he points out that the accused " says Christ was a Puritan, in his Index." Noy calls it an index, but Prynne himself describes it as "A Table (with some brief additions) of the chiefest passages in this treatise." *

* There is a note to the table which shows

The entries in the index are so curious
and one-sided in their accusations that
it is worth while to quote some of them
rather fully :

" Actors of popular or private enterludes
for gaine or pleasure, infamous, unlawfull
and that as well in Princes, Noblemen,
Gentlemen, Schollers, Divines or Common
Actors."

" Æschylus, one of the first inventors
of Tragedies—his strange and sudden
death."

" Christ wept oft, but never laughed—
a puritan—dishonoured and offended
with Stage playes."

" Crossing of the face when men go
to plays shuts in the Devil."

" Devils, inventors and fomentors of
stage plays and dancing.   Have stage
plays in hell every Lord's day night."

" Heaven—no stage plays there."

that the book grew in size during the printing—
" p. signifying the page, f. the folioes from
pag. 513 to 545 (which exceeded the Printer's
computation), m. the marginall notes : if you
finde f. before any pages from 545 to 568, then
looke the folioes which are overcast ; if p. then
the page following."

" Herod Agrippa smitten in theater by an angel and so died."

" Herod the great, the first erecter of a theater among the Jews who thereupon conspire his death."

" King James his statute against prophaning scripture and God's name in Playes—his Statutes make Players rogues and Playes unlawfull pastimes."

" Kings—infamous for them to act or frequent Playes or favour Players."

" Plagues occasioned by stage plays. All the Roman actors consumed by a plague."

" Play-bookes see Bookes."

" Players infamous . . .

——many of them Papists and most desperate wicked wretches."

" Play haunters the worst and lewdest persons for the most part . . ."

" Play haunting unlawfull . . ."

" Play-houses stiled by the Fathers and others, the Devil's temples, Chappels and synagogues . . ."

" Play-poets examples of God's judgements on the chiefest of them . . ."

" Puritans, condemners of Stage-plays and other corruptions stiled so—The

very best and holiest Christians called
so . . . —Christ, his prophets, apostles,
the Fathers and Primitive christians
Puritans as men now judged—hated
and condemned onely for their grace yea
holinesse of life—Accused of hypocrisie
and sedition, and why."

" Puritan, an honourable nickname of
Christianity and grace."

" Theaters overturned by tempests."

It was the strong terms in which women
actors are denounced that gave such
offence at Court, where the Queen and
her ladies were specially attracted to the
stage. Prynne's book was published six
weeks before Henrietta Maria acted in
a pastoral at Somerset House, so that
the following passage could not have
been intended to allude to the Queen : *

"Women actors notorious whores . . .
and dare then any Christian women be
so more than whorishly impudent as to
act, to speake publikely on a stage perchance in man's apparell and cut haire
here proved sinfull and abominable in

* See Cobbett's *State Trials*, vol. 3, coll.
561–586.

the presence of sundry men and women ?
. . . O let such presidents of impudency,
of impiety be never heard of or suffered
among Christians."

There are some interesting letters in
Ellis's *Original Letters* (2nd Series, vol. 3)
which illustrate the effect on the Court
of these violent expressions of opinion.
Jo. Pory wrote to Sir Thomas Puckering
on September 20th, 1632 : " That which
the Queen's Majesty, some of her ladies
and all her maides of honour are now
practicing upon is a Pastorall penned
by Mr. Walter Montague, wherein her
Majesty is pleased to acte a parte, as
well for her recreation as for the exercise
of her Englishe."

George Gresley wrote to the same
Puckering on the following 31st of
January : " Mr. Prinne an Utter Barrister
of Lincoln's Inne is brought into the
High Commission Court and Star
Chamber, for publishing a Booke (a
little before the Queene's acting of her
play) of the unlawfullness of Plaies
wherein in the Table of his Booke and
his brief additions thereunto he hath

these words [the extracts given above are here printed], which wordes it is thought by some will cost him his eares, or heavily punnisht and deepely fined."

Those who thought thus were amply justified in their opinion. Mr. Hill Burton observes that it was a very odd compliment to Queen Henrietta Maria to presume that these words refer to her, and he adds that the supposition reminds him of Victor Hugo's sarcasm respecting Napoleon III., that when the Parisian police overheard any one use the terms "ruffian" and "scoundrel," they said, "You must be speaking of the Emperor!"

Prynne is so full in his particulars that he might have given us much information respecting the stage in his own day, which we should have welcomed ; but, instead, he is ever more ready to draw his examples from Greek and Latin authorities.

In the eighteenth century a practice arose of drawing up indexes of sentiments and opinions as distinguished from facts. Such indexes required a special skill in the indexer, who was usually the original

author. There is a curious poetical index
to the Iliad in Pope's *Homer*, referring to
all the places in which similes are used.

Samuel Johnson was very anxious that
Richardson should produce such an index
to his novels. In the *Correspondence of
Samuel Richardson* (vol. v., p. 282) is
a letter from Johnson to the novelist,
in which he writes: " I wish you would
add an *index rerum*, that when the reader
recollects any incident, he may easily
find it, which at present he cannot do,
unless he knows in which volume it is
told; for Clarissa is not a performance
to be read with eagerness, and laid aside
for ever ; but will be occasionally consulted
by the busy, the aged and the studious ;
and therefore I beg that this edition, by
which I suppose posterity is to abide, may
want nothing that can facilitate its use."

At the end of each volume of *Clarissa
Harlowe* Richardson added a sort of
table of all the passages best worth
remembering, and as he was the judge
himself, it naturally extended to a considerable length. In September, 1753,
Johnson again wrote to Richardson

suggesting the propriety of making an index to his three works, but he added : "While I am writing an objection arises ; such an index to the three would look like the preclusion of a fourth, to which I will never contribute; for if I cannot benefit mankind I hope never to injure them."

Richardson took the hint of his friend, and in 1755 appeared a volume of four hundred and ten pages, entitled, *A Collection of the moral and instructive Sentiments, Maxims, Cautions, and Reflexions contained in the Histories of Pamela, Clarissa and Sir Charles Grandisón, digested under proper heads.*"

The tables of sentiments are arranged in separate alphabets for each novel. The production of this book was a labour of love to its author, who, moreover, was skilled in the mechanical work of indexing, and in the early part of his career had filled up his leisure hours by compiling indexes for the booksellers and writing prefaces and dedications. At the end of his "collection" are two letters from the author to two of his admirers; one was to a lady who was

solicitous for an additional volume to
Sir Charles Grandison, supposing that
work ended too abruptly.

David Hume is to be added to the
list of celebrated men who have been
indexers, although he does not appear to
have liked the work. In referring to the
fourth edition of his *Essays* he wrote :
" I intend to make an index to it." Two
years later he is grateful that the work of
indexing another book is to be done for
him ; writing to Millar (December 18th,
1759), he says : " I think that an Index
will be very proper, and am glad that
you free me from the trouble of undertaking that task, for which I know myself
to be very unfit." *

Sir James Paget, the great surgeon, not
only made indexes, but delighted in the
task. He told Dr. Goodhart, *apropos* of
the Hunterian Museum Catalogues, College of Surgeons, that " it had always been
a pleasure to him to make an index."†

At the end of this chapter I must

* Letters of David Hume to William Strahan,
edited by G. Birkbeck Hill, D.C.L. Oxford, 1888.
† Paget's *Life*, p. 350.

refer to an excellent blunder, because it would not be fair to introduce it with the work of the bad indexer, as it is an instance not exactly of ignorance, but of too great cleverness.

Of the Fétis Musical Library, bought by the Belgian Government at his death for 152,000 francs, an excellent catalogue was compiled and printed. In the index are references to Dumas (Alexandre) *pere*, and Dumas (Alexandre) *fils*. The musician who consults the work will be surprised at this unexpected development of these two famous authors' powers, but will be disappointed on referring to the numbers cited to find that they are reports of some legal proceedings brought by the firm of Alexandre *pere et fils*, the well-known harmonium-makers, against a rival firm. The indexer's better acquaintance with *Les Trois Mousquetaires* and *La Dame aux Camélias* led him astray.

My friend Mr. J. E. Matthew, who communicated this to me, adds : " After many years of constant use of the catalogue, this is the only mistake, beyond a literal, that I ever found."

CHAPTER II.

Amusing and Satirical Indexes.

"It will thus often happen that the controversialist states his case first in the title-page ;
he then gives it at greater length in the introduction ; again perhaps in a preface ; a third time
in an analytical form through means of a table
of contents; after all this skirmishing he brings
up his heavy columns in the body of the book ; and
if he be very skilfull he may let fly a few Parthian
arrows from the index."—J. Hill Burton's
Book-Hunter.

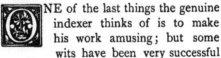NE of the last things the genuine
indexer thinks of is to make
his work amusing; but some
wits have been very successful
in producing humorous indexes, and
others have seen their way to make an
author ridiculous by satirically perverting
his meaning in the form of an ordinary
index. We can find specimens of each
of these classes.

Leigh Hunt has a charming little paper,
" A Word upon Indexes," in his *Indicator.*
He writes : " Index-making has been held
to be the driest as well as lowest species
of writing.   We shall not dispute the
humbleness of it ; but since we have had
to make an index ourselves,* we have
discovered that the task need not be
so very dry.   Calling to mind indexes in
general, we found them presenting us a
variety of pleasant memories and contrasts.
We thought of those to the Spectator,
which we used to look at so often at
school, for the sake of choosing a paper
to abridge.   We thought of the index
to the Pantheon of Fabulous Histories
of the Heathen Gods, which we used to
look at oftener.   We remember how we
imagined we should feel some day, if ever
our name should appear in the list of
Hs ; as thus, Home, Howard, Hume,
Huniades, ——.   The poets would have
been better, but then the names, though
perhaps less unfitting, were not so flatter-
ing ; as for instance Halifax, Hammond,

* To the original edition of the *Indicator*; the
reprint (2 vols. 8vo, 1834) has no index.

Harte, Hughes, ———. We did not like to
come after Hughes."

The indexes to the *Tatler* and the
Spectator are full of piquancy, and possess
that admirable quality of making the
consulter wish to read the book itself.
The entries are so enticing that they
lead you on to devour the whole book.
Hunt writes of them : "We have just
been looking at the indexes to the Tatler
and Spectator, and never were more
forcibly struck with the feeling we
formerly expressed about a man's being
better pleased with other writers than
with himself. Our index seemed the
poorest and most second-hand in the
world after theirs : but let any one read
theirs, and then call an index a dry thing
if he can. As there ' is a soul of goodness in things evil ' so there is a soul of
humour in things dry, and in things dry
by profession. Lawyers know this, as
well as index-makers, or they would die
of sheer thirst and aridity. But as grapes,
ready to burst with wine, issue out of
the most stony places, like jolly fellows
bringing burgundy out of a cellar ; so an

Index, like the *Tatler's,* often gives us a
taste of the quintessence of his humour."
The very title gives good promise of
what is to be found in the book: "A
faithful Index of the dull as well as the
ingenious passages in the Tatlers."

Here are a few entries chosen at random:
Vol. 1—
" Bachelor's scheme to govern a wife."
" Knaves prove fools."
Vol. 2—
"Actors censured for adding words of
their own in their parts."
" Dead men, who."
"Dead persons heard, judged and
censured.
——— Allegations laid against them,
their pleas."
" Love letters before and after marriage,
found in a grave."
" Mathematical sieve to sift impertin-
ences in writing and discourse."
" News, Old People die in France."
Vol. 3—
"Flattery of women, its ill conse-
quences."
" Maids of Honour, their allowance

of Beef for their Breakfast in Queen
Elizabeth's time."

"Silence, significant on many occasions.

—— Instances of it."

Vol. 4—

"Blockheads apt to admire one
another."

"Female Library proposed for the Improvement of the Sex."

"Night, longer formerly in this Island
than at present."

In 1757 *A General Index to the
Spectators, Tatlers, and Guardians* was
published, and in 1760 the same work
was re-issued with a new title-page.
Certain supposed blots in the original
indexes were here corrected and the
following explanation made in the preface :
"Notwithstanding the learning and care
of the compilers of the first Indexes to
these volumes, some slight inaccuracies
have passed, and where observed they
are altered. Few readers who desire to
know Mr. Bickerstaff's Opinion of the
Comedy called the Country Wife, or the
character of Mrs. Bickerstaff as an actress,
would consult the Index under the word

Acts." This seems to refer to an entry in
the index to the first volume of the *Tatler* :
   " Acts the Country-Wife : (Mrs. Bignel)."
   The index to the original edition of the
Spectator is equally good with that of
the *Tatler*, but the entries are longer and
more elaborate than those in the latter.
The references are not made to the pages,
as is the case with the *Tatler*, but to the
numbers of the papers.   The following
entries are worthy of quotation :
   Vol. 2—
   " Gentry of England generally speaking
in debt."
   " Great men not truly known till some
years after their deaths."
   " Women, the English excel all other
nations in beauty.
   —— Signs of their improvement under
the Spectator's hands.
   —— Their pains in all ages to adorn
the outside of their heads."
   A precursor of the *Tatler* and *Spectator*
was the curious *Athenian Oracle,* of the
eccentric John Dunton, each volume of
which contained " An Alphabetical Table
for the speedy finding of any questions,

by a member of the Athenian Society,"
from which the following amusing entries
are taken :

"Ark, what became of it after the
Flood ? "

" Bees, a swarm lit upon the Crown
and Scepter in Cheapside, what do they
portend ? "

" Hawthorn-tree at Glassenbury, what
think you of it ? "

" Noah's flood, whither went the
waters ? "

" Pied Piper, was he a man or dæmon ?"

"Triumphant Arch erected in Cheapside
1691, described."

A selection from this curious seven-
teenth-century miscellany was made by
Mr. J. Underhill, and published by
Walter Scott a few years ago.

Shenstone's *Schoolmistress* is one of the
works of genius which is little known in
the present day, but well repays perusal.
A humorous table of contents was
prepared by the author, which he styled
an index. He wrote : " I have added a
ludicrous index purely to show (fools)
that I am in jest." This was afterwards

omitted, but D'Israeli reprinted it in his *Curiosities of Literature.* It contains an amusing *précis* of the chief points of the poem ; the whole is short, and a few extracts will give an idea of its plan :

" A CIRCUMSTANCE in the situation of the mansion of early Discipline, discovering the surprising influence of the connexion of ideas."

" SOME peculiarities indicative of a country school, with a short sketch of the sovereign presiding over it."

" SOME account of her night-cap, apron and a tremendous description of her birchen sceptre."

" HER titles and punctilious nicety in the ceremonious assertion of them."

" A VIEW of this rural potentate as seated in her chair of state, conferring honours distributing bounties and dispensing proclamations."

Gay composed a full and humorous index for his interesting picture of eighteenth-century London—*Trivia.* The poet added a few entries to the index in the quarto edition of his *Poems* (1720). The following selected references will show the character of the index :

" Asses, their arrogance."

" Autumn, what cries then in use."

" Bully, his insolence to be corrected."

" Chairs and chariots prejudicial to health."

" Cellar, the misfortune of falling into one."

" Coach fallen into a hole described."

" Glazier, his skill at football."

" London, its happiness before the invention of Coaches and Chairs."

" Periwigs, how stolen off the head."

" Quarrels for the wall to be avoided."

" Schoolboys, mischievous in frosty weather."

" Wall, to whom to be given.

—— to whom to be denied."

" Women, the ill consequence of gazing on them."

Of modern examples of the amusing index, by far the best is that added to the inimitable *Biglow Papers* by the accomplished author, James Russell Lowell. Here are some extracts from the index to the First Series :

" Adam, eldest son of, respected."

" Babel, probably the first congress."

3

" Birch, virtue of, in instilling certain of the dead languages."

"Cæsar, a tribute to. His *Veni, Vidi, Vici* censured for undue prolixity."

" Castles, Spanish, comfortable accommodation in."

" Eating Words, habit of, convenient in time of famine."

"Longinus recommends swearing (Fuseli did the same thing)."

" No, a monosyllable. Hard to utter."

" Noah enclosed letter in bottle, probably."

" Ulysses, husband of Penelope. Borrows money. (For full particulars see *Homer* and *Dante*.)"

" Wrong, abstract, safe to oppose."

The following are from the Second Series:

" Antony of Padua, Saint, happy in his hearers."

" Applause, popular, the *summum bonum*."

" ' Atlantic,' editors of, See *Neptune*. [There is no entry under Neptune.] "

" Belmont. See *Woods*."

" Bible, not composed for use of coloured persons."

" Charles I, accident to his neck."

" Ezekiel would make a poor figure at a Caucus."

" Facts, their unamiability. Compared to an old fashioned stage-coach."

" Family trees, a primitive forest of."

" Jeremiah hardly the best guide in modern politics."

" Missionaries, useful to alligators. Culinary liabilities of."

" Rum and water combine kindly."

" Shoddy, poor covering for outer or inner man."

" ' They'll say,' a notable bully."

" Woods, the, See *Belmont.*"

" World, this, its unhappy temper."

" Writing, dangerous to reputation."

The witty Dr. William King, student of Christ Church, Oxford, and afterwards Judge of the Irish Court of Admiralty, presented an example of the skilled controversialist spoken of by Hill Burton as letting fly " a few Parthian arrows from the Index." He was dubbed by Isaac D'Israeli the inventor of satirical indexes, and he certainly succeeded in producing several ill-natured ones.

When the wits of Christ Church produced under the name of the Hon.
Charles Boyle the clever volume with
which they thought to annihilate the
great Dr. Bentley, Dr. King was the one
who assisted by producing a bitter index.

The first edition of *Dr. Bentley's
Dissertation on the Epistles of Phalaris
and the Fables of Esop examin'd* (1698)
has no index ; but Dr. King's work was
added to the second edition published
in the same year.   It was styled, *A
short account of Dr. Bentley by way of
Index.*   Then follows :

"Dr. Bentley's true story of the MS.
prov'd false by the testimonies of

—— Mr. Bennet, p. 6.

—— Mr. Gibson, p. 7.

—— Dr. King, p. 8.

—— Dr. Bentley, p. 19."

" Dr. Bentley's civil usage of Mr. Boyle.

" His civil language to

—— Mr. Boyle.

—— Sir W. Temple.

" His singular humanity to

—— Mr. Boyle.

—— Sir Edward Sherburne.

humanity to Foreigners.

" His Ingenuity in

—— relating matters of fact.

—— citing authors.

—— transcribing and plundering notes and prefaces of

—— Mr. Boyle.

—— Vizzanius.

—— Nevelet.

—— Camerarius.

—— Editor of Hesychius.

—— Salmasius.

—— Dr. Bentley.

" His appeal to Foreigners.

—— a suspicious plan.

—— a false one.

" His modesty and decency in contradicting great men.

" (Long list from Plato to Every body).

" His happiness in confident assertions for want

—— of Reading.

—— of Judgment.

—— of Sincerity.

" His profound skill in Criticism

From beginning to

The End."

This is certainly more vindictive than witty.

All the wits rushed madly into the fray, and Swift, in his "Battel fought last Friday between the Antient and Modern Books in St. James's Library," committed himself irretrievably to the wrong side in this way: "A captain whose name was B-ntl-y, in person the most deformed of all the moderns; tall but without shape or comeliness, large but without strength or proportion. His armour was patched up of a thousand incoherent pieces . . ."

Then look at the leader of the opposing host: "Boyl clad in a suit of armor which had been given him by all the gods immediately advanced against the trembling foe, who now fled before him."

It is amazing that such a perverted judgment should have been given by some of our greatest writers, but all is to be traced to Bentley's defects of temper, so that Dr. King was not altogether wrong in his index.

Sir George Trevelyan in his *Life of Macaulay* refers to Bentley's famous maxim (which in print and talk alike

he dearly loved to quote), that no man
was ever written down except by himself,
and quotes what the historian wrote
after perhaps his tenth perusal of Bishop
Monk's life of the great critic : " Bentley
seems to me an eminent instance of the
extent to which intellectual powers of a
most rare and admirable kind may be
impaired by moral defects."

Charles Boyle's book went through four
editions, and still there was silence; but
at last appeared the "immortal" *Dissertation*, as Porson calls it, which not only
defeated his enemies, but routed them
completely. Bentley's *Dissertation upon
the Epistles of Phalaris*, with an answer
to the objections of the Hon. C.
Boyle, Esq., first appeared in 1699. De
Quincey described it as one of the
three most triumphant dissertations existing upon the class of historico-critical
problems, " All three are loaded with a
superfetation of evidence, and conclusive
beyond what the mind altogether wishes."*
In another place De Quincey points out

* *Rosicrucians and Free-Masons* (De Quincey's
Works, vol. 13, p. 388).

the line of argument followed by Bentley :
" It was by anachronisms of this character that Bentley detected the spuriousness
of the letters ascribed to Phalaris. Sicilian
towns, &c., were in those letters called
by names that did not arise until that
prince had been dead for centuries.
Manufactures were mentioned that were
of much later invention. As handles for
this exposure of a systematic forgery,
which oftentimes had a moral significance,
these indications were valuable, and gave
excessive brilliancy to that immortal dissertation of Bentley's." *

The fate which the wits thought to
bring upon Bentley fell upon them, and
they quarrelled among themselves. It
was believed that Charles Boyle, when
credit was to be obtained, looked upon
himself as author of the book ; but afterwards, when it was discredited, he only
awaited the public trial of the conspirators
to wash his hands of the whole affair.
Atterbury, who had much to do with the
production of the volume, was particularly

* *Memorial Chronology* (De Quincey's *Works*,
vol. 14, p. 309).

annoyed by Boyle's conduct. He wrote to Boyle : " In laying the design of the book, in writing above half of it, in reviewing [revising] a great part of the rest, in transcribing the whole and attending the press, half a year of my life went away. What I promised myself from hence was that some service would be done to your reputation, and that you would think so. In the first of these I was not mistaken—in the latter I am. When you were abroad, sir, the highest you could prevail with yourself to go in your opinion of the book was, that you hoped it would do you no harm. When you returned I supposed you would have seen that it had been far from hurting you. However, you have not thought fit to let me know your mind on this matter ; for since you came to England, no one expression, that I know of, has dropped from you that could give me reason to believe you had any opinion of what I had done, or even took it kindly from me." *

* *Memoirs of Bishop Atterbury,* compiled by Folkestone Williams, vol. i. (1869), p. 42.

In the same year (1698) King turned his attention to a less formidable antagonist than the great Bentley. His *Journey to London* is a very ingenious parody of Dr. Martin Lister's *Journey to Paris*, and, the pages of the original being referred to, it forms an index to that book.

The Royal Society in its early years had to pass through a long period of ridicule and misrepresentation. The author of *Hudibras* commenced the crusade, but the gibes of Butler were easier to bear than those of Dr. William King, who was particularly savage against Sir Hans Sloane. *The Transactioneer* (1700) and *Useful Transactions in Philosophy* (1708–1709) were very galling to the distinguished naturalist, and annoyed the Royal Society, whose *Philosophical Transactions* were unmercifully laughed at. To both the tracts referred to were prefixed satirical tables of contents, and what made them the more annoying was that the author's own words were very ingeniously used and turned against him. King writes : " The bulls and blunders

which Sloane and his friends so naturally
pour forth cannot be misrepresented, so
careful I am in producing them."

Here is a specimen of the contents
of *The Transactioneer* :

"The Tatler's Opinion of a Virtuoso."

" Some Account of Sir Hans Sloane.

—— of Dr. Salmon.

—— of Mr. Oldenburg.

—— of Dr. Plot."

" The Compiling of the Philosophical
Transactions the work of a single person.

—— the excellence of his style.

—— his clearness and perspicacity.

—— Genius to Poetry.

—— Verses on Jamaica Pepper.

—— Politicks in Gardening.

—— Skill in Botanicks."

The following appear in the contents
of the " Voyage to Cajamai " in *Useful
Transactions* :

Preface of the author—

" Knew a white bramble in a dark
room."

Author's introduction—

" Mountains higher than hills."

" Hay good for horses."

The most important of King's indexes was that added to Bromley's *Travels,* because it had the effect of balking a distinguished political character of his ambition of filling the office of Speaker of the House of Commons.

William Bromley (1664–1732), after leaving Christ Church, Oxford, spent several years in travelling on the Continent. He was elected a Member of Parliament in 1689, and soon occupied a prominent position among the nonjurors. In 1692 he published "*Remarks in the Grande Tour of France and Italy, lately performed by a Person of quality.* London. Printed by E. H. for Tho. Basset at the George in Fleet Street, 1692." A second edition appeared in the following year: "*Remarks made in Travels through France and Italy, with many Publick Inscriptions. Lately taken by a Person of Quality.* London (Thomas Basset) 1693."

In March, 1701–1702, Bromley was electedMember of Parliament for the University of Oxford, which he continued to represent during the remainder of his life.

In 1702 he published another volume of travels: "*Several Years' Travels through Portugal, Spain, Italy, Germany, Prussia, Sweden, Denmark and the United Provinces performed by a Gentleman.*"

In 1705 Bromley was supposed to have pre-eminent claims to the Speakership, which office was then vacant ; but what was supposed to be a certainty was turned into failure by the action of his opponents. They took the opportunity of reprinting his *Remarks*, with the addition of a satirical index, as an electioneering squib. This reprint appeared as " *Remarks in the Grand Tour . . . performed by a Person of Quality in the year* 1691. The second edition to which is added a table of the principal matters. London. Printed for John Nutt near Stationers' Hall, 1705." This was really the third edition, but probably the reprinters overlooked the edition of 1693. It was reprinted with the original licence of " Rob. Midgley, Feb. 20th, 1691–2."

In the Bodleian copy of this book there is a manuscript note by Dr. Rawlinson to the effect that this index was drawn up by

Robert Harley, Earl of Oxford; but this
was probably only a party rumour. Dr.
Parr possessed Bromley's own copy of
the reprint with the following manuscript
note by the author:

"This edition of these travels is a specimen of the good nature and good manners
of the Whigs, and I have reason to believe of one of the ministry (very con-
versant in this sort of calumny) for the
sake of publishing '*the Table of the principal matters &c*' to expose me whom
the gentlemen of the Church of England
designed to be Speaker of the House
of Commons, in the Parliament, that
met Oct. 25 1705. When notwithstanding the Whigs and Court joining
to keep me out of the chair, and the
greatest violence towards the Members,
turning out some, and threatening others,
to influence their votes, I had the
honour (and I shall ever esteem it a
greater honour than my competitor's
success) to have the suffrages of 205
disinterested gentlemen for me : such a
number as never lost such a question
before ; and such as, with the addition

of those that by force, and contrary to
their inclination, with the greatest re-
luctance voted against me, must have
prevailed for me.

"This was a very malicious proceeding;
my words and meaning plainly perverted
in several places; which if they had been
improper, and any observations trifling or
impertinent, an allowance was due for
my being very young, when they were
made. But the performances of others,
not entitled to such allowance may be
in this manner exposed, as appears by
the like Tables published for the Travels
of Bp. Burnet and Mr. Addison. *Wm.
Bromley.*"

Dr. Parr took this all very seriously,
and set great value upon the book. He
added a note to that written by Bromley,
in which he said :

"Mr. Bromley was very much galled
with the republication, and the ridiculous,
but not untrue, representation of the
contents. Such a work would unavoid-
ably expose the author to derision :
instead therefore of suffering it to be
sold after my death, and to become a

subject of contemptuous gossip, or an instrument of party annoyance, I think it a proper act of respect and kindness for the Bromley family, for me to put it in possession of the Rev. Mr. Davenport Bromley, upon the express condition that he never sells it nor gives it away, that, after reading it, he seals it up carefully and places it where no busy eye, nor thievish hand can reach it.

"S. P."

This note was written in 1823, and the precautions taken by Parr seem rather belated. Even the family were little likely to mind the public seeing a political skit more than a century old, which did no dishonour to their ancestor's character.

It is very probable that Harley was at the expense of reprinting the book, as it is reported that every one who came to his house was asked if he had seen Mr. Bromley's *Travels*; and when the answer was in the negative, Harley at once fetched a copy, which he presented to his visitor. There is no doubt, however, that the index was drawn up by Dr. King.

The index is neither particularly amusing nor clever, but it is very ill-natured. Dr. Parr infers that the book is not misrepresented, but there can be little doubt that the index is in most instances very unfair. Thus the first entry in the table is :

" Chatham, where and how situated, viz. on the other side of Rochester bridge, though commonly reported to be on this side, p. 1."

The passage indexed is quite clear, and contains the natural statement of a fact.

"Lodged at Rochester, an episcopal seat in the same county [Kent]. The cathedral church is plain and decent, and the city appears well peopled. When I left it and passed the Bridge I was at Chatham, the famous Dock, where so many of our great ships are built."

The following are some further entries from the index :

" Dover and Calais neither of them places of Strength tho' frontier towns, p. 2."

" Boulogne the first city on the French shore, lies on the coast, p. 2." [These are the same words as in the book.]

4

" Crosses and Crucifixes on the Roads in France prove it not England, p. 3."

The passage here indexed is as follows :

" Crosses and Crucifixes are so plentiful every where on this road, that from them alone an Englishman will be satisfied he is out of his own country; besides the Roads are much better than ours."

" Eight pictures take up less room than sixteen of the same size, p. 14."

This is founded on the following :

" They contain the Histories of the Old and New Testaments, and are placed in two rows one above the other; those that represent the Old Testament are in the uppermost reaching round the room and are sixteen. Those of the new are under them, but being only eight reach not so far as the former, and where no pictures are be the doors to the presses where the sacred vestments are kept."

" Travelling by night not proper to take a view of the adjacent countries, p. 223."

This is a version of the following :

" The heat of the weather made

travelling in the night most desirable
and we chose it between Sienna and
Florence. . . . By this means I could see
little of the country."

" The Duchess dowager of Savoy who
was grandmother to the present Duke was
mother to his father, p. 243."

This is a perversion of the following
perfectly natural observation :

" This was designed by the Dutchess
Christina grandmother of this Duke in
the minority of her son (his father) in
1660."

The entry, " Jews at Legorn not obliged
to wear red hats, p. 223," contains nothing
absurd, but rather is an interesting piece
of information, because the Jews were
obliged to wear these hats in other parts
of Italy, and it was the knowledge of
this fact that induced Macklin to wear a
red hat when acting Shylock, a personation
which induced an admirer to exclaim :

> "This is the Jew
> That Shakespeare drew."

Such perversions as these could have
done Bromley, one would think, little

harm; but the real harm done consisted in bringing to light and insisting upon the author's political attitude when he referred to King William and Queen Mary as "the Prince and Princess of Orange." The passage is as follows:

"A gallery, where among the pictures of Christian Princes are those of King Charles the Second and his Queen, King James the Second and his Queen and the Prince and Princess of Orange."

It would indeed seem strange that one who had thus referred to his King and Queen should occupy so important a public office as Speaker of the House of Commons. Another ground of offence was that when in Rome he kissed the Pope's slipper.

Although Bromley was disappointed in 1705, his time came; and after the Tory reaction consequent on the trial of Sacheverell he was in 1710 chosen Speaker without opposition. There is a portrait of Bromley in the University Picture Gallery in the Bodleian at Oxford.

CHAPTER III.

The Bad Indexer.

"At the laundress's at the Hole in the Wall in Cursitor's Alley up three pair of stairs, the author of my Church history—you may also speak to the gentleman who lies by him in the flock bed, my index maker."—Swift's *Account of the Condition of Edmund Curll* (Instructions to a porter how to find Mr. Curll's authors).

BAD indexers are everywhere, and what is most singular is that each one makes the same sort of blunders—blunders which it would seem impossible that any one could make, until we find these same blunders over and over again in black and white. One of the commonest is to place the references under unimportant words, for which no one would think of looking, such as A and The. The worst indexes of this class are often added to journals

53

and newspapers. A good instance of
confusion will be found in the index to a
volume of *The Freemason* which is before
me ; but this is by no means singular,
and certainly not the worst of its class.
Under A we find the following entries :

" Afternoon Outing of the Skelmersdale
Lodge."

" An Oration delivered," etc.

" Annual Outing of the Queen Victoria
Lodge."

" Another Masonic MS."

Under B :

" Bro. Bain's Masonic Library."

Under F :

" First Ball of the Fellowship Lodge.

" First Ladies' Night."

Under I :

" Interesting Extract from an 'Old
Masonian's ' Letter."

Under L :

" Ladies' Banquet."

" Ladies' Night."

" Ladies' Summer Outing."

" Late Bro. Sir B. W. Richardson."

Under N :

" New Grand Officers."

" New Home for Keighley Freemasons."
" New Masonic Hall."
Under O :
" Our Portrait Gallery."
Under R :
" Recent Festival."
Under S :
" Send-off dinner."
"Summer Festival."
" Summer Outing."
Under T :
" Third Ladies' Night."
Under Y :
" Ye olde Masonians."
There are many other absurd headings,
but these are the worst instances. They
show the confusion of not only placing
references where they would never be
looked for, but of giving similar entries
all over the index under whatever heading
came first to the mind of the indexer. For
instance, there is one *Afternoon* Outing,
one *Annual* Outing, one *Ladies'* Outing,
one *Summer* Outing, and three other
Outings under O. None of these have
any references the one from the other.
There are a large number of indexes

in which not only the best heading is not chosen, but the very worst is. Thus, choosing at random, we find such an order as the following in an old volume of the *Canadian Journal* :

"*A* Monograph of the British Spongiadæ."

"*On* the Iodide of Barium."

"*Sir* Charles Barry, a Biography."

"*The* late Professor Boole."

"*The* Mohawk Language."

The same misarrangement will sometimes be found even in standard English journals.

The edition of Jewel's *Apology*, published by Isaacson in 1825, contains an index which is worthy of special remark. It is divided into four alphabets, referring respectively to (1) Life ; (2) Apology ; (3) Notes to Life ; (4) Notes to Apology ; and this complicated machinery is attached to a book of only 286 pages. I think it is scarcely too much to say that there is hardly an entry in the index which would be of any use to the consulter. A few examples will show that this is not an unfair judgment :

"*Belief* of a Resurrection."

"*Caution*, Reformers proceeded with Caution."

"*If* Protestants are Heretics let the Papists prove them so from Scripture."

"*In* withdrawing themselves from the Church of Rome, Protestants have not erred from Christ and his Apostles."

"*King* John."

"*The* Pope assumes Regal power and habit."

"Ditto employs spies."

That this idiotic kind of index (which can be of no possible use to any one) is not yet extinct may be seen in one of those daintily printed books of essays which are now so common. In mercy I will not mention the title, but merely say that it was published in 1901. A few extracts will show the character of the work:

"*A* Book," etc.

"*Is* public taste," etc.

"*On* reading old books."

"*The* advantage," etc.

"*The* blessedness," etc.

"*The* Book-stall Reader."

"*The* Girl," etc.

" *The* Long Life," etc.

" *The* Preservative," etc.

" *The* Prosperity," etc.

" *Two* Classes of Literature.

There are many instances of such bad indexes, but it would be tedious to quote more of them. The amazing thing is that many persons unconnected with one another should be found to do the same ridiculous work, and suppose that by any possibility it could be of use to a single human being. But what is even more astounding is to find intelligent editors passing such useless rubbish and wasting good type and paper upon it.

Another prominent blunder in indexing periodicals is to follow in the index the divisions of the paper. In an alphabetical index there should be no classification, but the alphabet should be followed throughout. Nothing is so maddening to consult as an index in which the different divisions of the periodical are kept distinct, with a separate alphabet under each. It is hopeless to consult these, and it is often easier to turn over the pages and look through the volume than to refer to the index. The main object of an index is to bring together all the items on a similar subject which are separated in the book itself.

The indexes of some periodicals are good, but those of the many are bad. Mr. Poole and his helpers, who had an extensive experience of periodical literature, made the following rule to be observed in the new edition of Poole's *Index to Periodical Literature* :

"All references must be made from an inspection, and if necessary the perusal of each article. Hence, no use will be made of the index which is usually printed with the volume, or of any other index. Those indexes were *made by unskilful persons*, and are full of all sorts of errors. It will be less work to discard them entirely than to supply their omissions and correct their errors."

This rule is sufficiently severe, but it cannot be said that it is unjust.

Miss Hetherington, who has had a singularly large experience of indexes to periodicals, has no higher idea of these than Mr. Poole. In an article on "The

Indexing of Periodicals " in the *Index to the Periodical Literature of the World* for 1892, she gives a remarkable series of instances of absurd entries. Some of these are due to the vicious habit of trying to save trouble by cutting up the lists of contents, and repeating the entries under different headings. Miss Hetherington's examples are well worth repeating; but as bad indexing is the rule, it is scarcely worth while to gibbet any one magazine, as most of them are equally bad. It is only amazing how any one in authority can allow such absurdities as the following to be printed. These six groups are from one magazine:

" Academy in Africa, A Monkey's."

" Africa, A Monkey's Academy in."

" Monkey's Academy in Africa, A."

" Aspects, The Renaissance in its Broader."

" Renaissance in its Broader Aspects, The."

" Campaign, His Last, and After."

" His Last Campaign, and After."

" Entertainment, The Triumph of the Variety."

" Triumph of the Variety Entertainment, The."

" Variety Entertainment, The Triumph of the."

" Evicted Tenants, The Irish, Are they Knaves ? "

" Irish Evicted Tenants, The, Are they Knaves ? "

" French Revolution, Scenes from the."

" Revolution, Scenes from the French."

" Scenes from the French Revolution."

Miss Hetherington adds, respecting this particular magazine : " But the whole index might be quoted. The indexer seems to have had three lists of contents for his purpose, but he has not always dared to use more than two, and so " The Irish Evicted Tenants " do not figure under the class " Knaves." The contributors are on another page, with figures only against their names, the cause of reference not being specified."

Equally absurd, and contrived on a similar system, are the following entries from another magazine :

" Eastern Desert on Foot, Through an."

" Foot, Through an Eastern Desert on."

"Through an Eastern Desert on Foot."

"Finds, The Rev. J. Sturgis's."

"Sturgis's Finds, The Rev. J."

"Complexion! What a Pretty."

"Pretty Complexion! What a."

"What a Pretty Complexion!"

These two groups are from a very prominent magazine:

"Creek in Demerara, Up a."

"Demerara, Up a Creek in."

"Up a Creek in Demerara."

"Home, The Russians at."

"Russians at Home, The."

"The Russians at Home."

In the foregoing, by giving three entries, one, by chance, may be correct; but in the following case there are two useless references:

"Baron de Marbot, The Memoirs of the."

"Memoirs of the Baron de Marbot, The."

But nothing under *Marbot.*

Some indexers have a fancy for placing authors under their Christian names, as these three from one index.

"Philip Bourke Marston."

" Rudyard Kipling."

" Walt Whitman."

These entries are amusing :

" Foot in it, On Putting One's."

" On Putting One's Foot in it."

Surely it is strange that such absurdities as these should continue to be published ! Mr. Poole drew attention to the evil, and Miss Hetherington has done the same ; yet it continues, and publishers are not ashamed to print such rubbish as that just instanced. We may add a quite recent instance—viz. *Longman's Magazine* for October, 1901, which contains an index to the thirty-eighth volume. It occupies two pages in double columns, and there are no duplicate entries. In that small space I find these useless entries :

" According to the Code " (not under Code).

" Disappearance of Plants " (not under Plants).

" Eighteenth Century London through French Eye-glasses " (not under London).

" Gilbert White " (not under White).

" Mission of Mr. Rider Haggard " (not under Haggard).

" Some Eighteenth Century Children's Books " (not under Children's Books).

" Some Notes on an Examination " (not under Examination).

The two chief causes of the badness of indexes are found—

1. In the original composition.

2. In the bad arrangement.

Of the first cause little need be said. The chief fault is due to the incompetence of the indexer, shown by his use of trivial references, his neglect of what should be indexed, his introduction of what might well be left out, his bad analysis, and his bad headings.

The second cause is still more important, because a competent indexer may prepare his materials well, and keep clear of all the faults noticed above, and yet spoil his work by neglect of a proper system of arrangement.

The chief faults under this second division consist of—

1. Want of complete alphabetisation.

2. Classification within the alphabet.

3. Variety of alphabets.

4. Want of cross references.

These are all considerable faults, and will therefore bear being enlarged upon.

1. *The want of complete alphabetisation* is a great evil, but it was very general at one time. In some old indexes references are arranged under the first letter only. In the index to a large and valuable map of England, published at the beginning of this century, the names of places are not arranged further than the third letter, and this naturally gives great trouble to the consulter. In order to save himself, the compiler has given others a considerably greater amount of trouble. In arranging entries in alphabetical order it is necessary to sort them to the most minute difference of spelling. The alphabetical arrangement, however, has its difficulties, which must be overcome; for instance, it looks awkward when the plural comes before the singular, and the adjective before the substantive from which it is formed, as "naval" and "navies" before "navy." In such cases it will be necessary to

5

make a heading such as " Navy," which
will include the plural and the adjective.

The vowel I should be kept distinct
from the consonant J, and the vowel U
from the consonant V.

More blunders have probably been
made by the confusing of u and n in
old books than from any other cause.
These letters are identical in early manuscripts, and consequently the modern
copyist has to decide which letter to
choose, and sometimes he blunders.

In Capgrave's *Chronicles of England*
is a reference to the "londe of Iude,"
but this is misspelt "Inde" in the edition
published in the Master of the Rolls'
Series in 1858. Here is a simple mis-
print caused by the misreading of I for J
and n for u ; but this can easily be set
right. The indexer, however, has enlarged it into a wonderful blunder.
Under the letter I is the following curious
piece of information :

" India . . . conquered by Judas Mac-
cabeus and his brethren, 56 " ! !

Many more instances of this confusion
of the letters u and n might be given,

some of them causing permanent confusion of names; but two (which are the complement of each other) will suffice.

George London was a very eminent horticulturist in his day, who at the Revolution was appointed Superintendent of the Royal Gardens; but he can seldom get his name properly spelt because a later horticulturist has made the name of Loudon more familiar. In fact, I was once called to account by a reviewer who supposed I had made a mistake in referring to London instead of Loudon. The reverse mistake was once made by the great Duke of Wellington. C. J. Loudon (who wrote a very bad hand) requested the Duke to let him see the Waterloo beeches at Stratfieldsaye. The letter puzzled Wellington, who knew nothing of the horticulturist, and read C. J. Loudon as C. J. London, and beeches as breeches; so he wrote off to the then Bishop of London (Dr. Blomfield) to say that his Waterloo breeches disappeared long ago.

2. *Classification within the alphabet.—* Examples have already been given where

the arrangement of the book is followed
rather than the alphabetical order ; but
these were instances of bad indexing,
and sometimes a good indexer fails in the
same way, thus showing how important
is good arrangement. An index of
great complexity, one full of scientific
difficulties, was once made by a very able
man. The *précis* was admirable, and the
various subjects were gathered together
under their headings with great skill
—in fact, it could not well have been
more perfect ; but it had one flaw which
spoiled it. The nature of the index
necessitated a large number of subdivisions under the various chief headings ;
these were arranged on a system clear
to the compiler, and probably a logical
one to him. But the user of the index
had not the clue to this arrangement,
and he could not find his way through
the complicated maze; it was an unfor-
tunate instance of extreme cleverness.
When the index was finished, but be
fore it was published, a simple remedy
for the confusion was suggested and
carried out. The whole of the sub-

divisions under each main heading were rearranged in perfect alphabetical order. This was a heroic proceeding, but it was highly successful, and the rearranged index gave satisfaction, and the same system was followed in other indexes that succeeded it.

3. *Variety of alphabets.*—An index should be one and indivisible, and should not be broken up into several alphabets. Foreigners are greater sinners against this fundamental rule than Englishmen, and they almost invariably separate the author or persons from subjects. Sometimes, however, the division is not very carefully made, for in the *Autoren Register* to Carus' and Engelmann's *Bibliography of Zoology* may be found the following entries : *Schreiben, Schriften, Zu* Humboldt's Cosmos, *Zur* Fauna. Some English books are much divided. Thus the new edition of Hutchins's *Dorset* (1874) has at the end eight separate indexes : (1) Places, (2) Pedigrees, (3) Persons, (4) Arms, (5) Blazons, (6) Glossarial, (7) Domesday, (8) Inquisitions.

The index to the original quarto edition
of Warton's *History of English Poetry*
(1774) has six alphabets, but a general
index compiled by Thomas Fillingham,
was published in 1804, uniform with the
work in quarto. The general index to
the *Annual Register* has as many as four-
teen alphabets. The general index to
the *Reports of the British Association* is
split up into six alphabets, following the
divisions of each volume.

4. *Want of cross references.*—Although
an alphabetical index should not be
classified, yet it is necessary to gather
together the synonyms, and place all
the references under the best of these
headings, with cross references from the
others. For instance, Wealth should be
under W, Finance under F, and Population under P ; and they should not all
be grouped under Political Economy,
because each of these subjects is distinct
and more conveniently found under the
separate heading than under a grouped
heading. On the other hand, entries
relating to Tuberculosis must not be scat-
tered over the index under such headings

as Consumption, Decline, and Phthisis, but be gathered together under the heading chosen, with cross references from the others. In bad indexes this rule is invariably broken, and it must be allowed that the proper carrying out of this rule is very difficult, so that where it is invariably adopted, we have one of the best signs of a really good index. Bad indexers are usually much too haphazard in their work to insert cross references.

The careful use of cross references is next in importance to the selection of appropriate headings. Great judgment, however, is required, as the consulters are naturally irritated by being referred backwards and forwards, particularly in a large index. At the same time, if judiciously inserted, such references are a great help. Mr. Poole says, in an article on his own index in the *Library Journal*: "If every subject shall have cross references to its allies, the work will be mainly a book of cross references rather than an index of subjects." He then adds: "One correspondent gives

fifty-eight cross references under Mental
Philosophy, and fifty-eight more might
be added just as appropriate."

The indexer should be careful that his
cross references are real, but he has not
always attended to this. In Eadie's *Dictionary of the Bible* (1850) there is a
reference, "Dorcas *see* Tabitha," but
there is no entry under Tabitha at all.

In Cobbett's *Woodlands* there is a good
specimen of backwards and forwards
cross referencing. The author writes :

"Many years ago I wished to know
whether I could raise birch trees from
the *seed.* . . . I then looked into the
great book of knowledge, the *Encyclopædia
Britannica* ; there I found in the general
dictionary :

"'BIRCH TREE— See *Betula* (Botany
Index).'

"I hastened to BETULA with great
eagerness, and there I found :

"'BETULA—Seè *Beech tree.*'

"That was all, and this was pretty
encouragement."

William Morris used to make merry
over the futility of some cross references.

He was using a print of an old English manuscript which was full of notes in explanation of self-evident passages, but one difficult expression—*viz.* "The bung of a thrub chandler "—was left unexplained. In the index under Bung there was a reference to Thrub chandler, and under Thrub chandler another back to Bung Still the lexicographers are unable to tell us what kind of a barrel a "thrub chandler " really was. I give this story on the authority of my friend, Mr. S. C. Cockerell.

No reference to the contents of a general heading which is without subdivision should be allowed unless of course the page is given.

There are too many vague cross references in the *Penny Cyclopædia* where you are referred from the known to the unknown. If a general heading be divided into sections, and each of these be clearly defined, they should be cross referenced, but not otherwise. At present you may look for Pesth and be referred to Hungary, where probably there is much about Pesth, but you do not know where to look for it in the long article without some clue. Sometimes cross references are mere expedients, particularly in the case of a cyclopædia published in volumes or parts. Thus a writer agrees to contribute an article early in the alphabet, but it is not ready in time for the publication of the part, so a cross reference is inserted which sends the reader to a synonym later on in the alphabet. In certain cases this has been done two or three times. An instance occurs in the life of the distinguished bibliographer, the late Henry Bradshaw (than whom no one was more capable of producing a masterly article), who undertook to write on "Printing" in the *Encyclopædia Britannica.* When the time for publication arrived (1885), Bradshaw was not ready, and in place of the article appeared the cross reference, "PRINTING, TYPOGRAPHIC—See *Typography.*" Bradshaw died on February 10, 1886, and the article on "Typography" which was published in Vol. 23 in 1888, was written by Mr. Hessels.

Cross referencing has its curiosities as well as other branches of our subject.

Perhaps the most odd collection of cross references is to be found in Serjeant William Hawkins's *Pleas of the Crown* (1716; 5th ed., 1771; 7th ed., 4 vols., 1795), of which it was said in the *Monthly Magazine* for June, 1801 (p. 419): "A plain, unlettered man is led to suspect that the writer of the volume and the writer of the index are playing at cross purposes."

The following are some of the most amusing entries :

" Cards *see* Dice. "

" Cattle *see* Clergy. "

" Chastity *see* Homicide. "

" Cheese *see* Butter. "

" Coin *see* High Treason. "

" Convicts *see* Clergy. "

" Death *see* Appeal. "

" Election *see* Bribery. "

"Farthings *see* Halfpenny. "

" Fear *see* Robbery. "

" Footway *see* Nuisance. "

" Honour *see* Constable. "

" Incapacity *see* Officers. "

" King *see* Treason. "

" Knaves *see* Words. "

" Letters *see* Libel."

" London *see* Outlawry."

'' Shop *see* Burglary."

" Sickness *see* Bail."

" Threats *see* Words."

" Westminster Hall *see* Contempt and Lie."

" Writing *see* Treason."

This arrangement of some of the cross references is perhaps scarcely fair. They are spread over several elaborate indexes in the original, and in their proper places do not strike one in the same way as when they are set out by themselves. One of the instances given by the critic in the *Monthly Magazine* is unfairly cited. It is there given as "Assault *see* Son." The cross reference really is, "Assault *see* Son Assault."

Hawkins's work is divided into two parts, and the folio editions have two indexes, one to each part ; the octavo edition has four indexes, one to each volume.

The index to Ford's *Handbook of Spain* contains an amusing reference :

" Wellington, *see* Duke."

Besides these four divisions of the chief faults in indexing, there are many other pitfalls gaping wide to receive the careless indexer.

Names are a great difficulty, but it is not necessary to refer to these more generally here, as they are fully dealt with in the rules (*see* Chapter VI.)

It is not often that an English indexer has to index a French book, but should he do so he would often need to be careful. The Frenchman does not care to leave that which he does not understand unexplained. The translation of *Love's Last Shift* as *La Derniere Chemise de l'Amour*, attributed by Horace Walpole to the Dowager Duchess of Bolton in George I.'s reign, is probably an invention, but some translations quite as amusing are genuine. G. Brunet of Bordeaux, having occasion in his *La France Litteraire au XVᵃ siècle* to mention "White Knights," at one time the seat of the Duke of Marlborough, translates it into *Le Chevalier Blanc.* When Dr. Buckland, the geologist, died, a certain French paper published a biography of him in which it was explained that the deceased had been a very versatile writer, for besides his work on geology he had produced one *Sur les Ponts et Chaussees.* This was a puzzling statement, but it turned out to be a translation of *Bridgewater Treatises*, in which series his *Geology and Mineralogy* was published in 1837.

Sometimes contractions give trouble to the indexer, and he must be careful not to fill them out unless he is sure of what they mean. Many blunders have been made in this way. In the *Historie of Edward IV.* (1471), edited by that careful and trustworthy antiquary John Bruce for the Camden Society in 1838, there is the following remarkable statement: "Wherefore the Kynge may say, as Julius Cæsar sayde, he that is not agaynst me is with me."

This chapter might be made a very long one by instancing a series of badly indexed books, but this would be a tedious recital devoid of any utility, for the blunders and carelessness of the bad indexer are singularly alike in their futility. It is nevertheless worth while to mention the index to Peter Cunningham's complete edition of Walpole's *Letters,* because that work deserves a good index. We may hope that when Mrs. Toynbee publishes her new and complete edition of the *Letters,* she will add a really satisfactory index. The present index is very bad and most irritating to the person who uses it. Examples of most of the careless and foolish blunders in indexing are to be found here ; for instance, there are long lists of references without indication of the reason for any of them. The same person is entered in two places if he is spoken of under slightly different names. The same nobleman is referred to as Lord —— and as the Earl of ——, while sometimes a heading devoted to Lord —— contains references to two distinct men. Van Eyck has one reference under Van and another under Eyck. Mrs. Godfrey is entered under both Godfrey and *La* Godfrey. Many other absurdities are to be found in the index, but the extract of one heading will be sufficient to show how ill the arrangement is :

" Gower, edition of,
—— Baptist Leveson,
—— Countess of,
—— Dowager Lady,
—— Duke of,
—— Earl of,
—— John, Earl,
—— Lady,
—— Lady Elizabeth,
—— Lady Mary Leveson,
—— Lord,
—— Richard Leveson."

There is no authority at all for a Duke of Gower, and if we look up the reference (iv. 39) we find that it refers to "the late Lord G——," possibly the Earl Gower.

The confusion by which two persons are made into one has sometimes an evil consequence worse than putting the consulter of an index on the wrong scent, for the character of an innocent person may be taken away by this means. (Constance) Lady Russell of Swallowfield points out in *Notes and Queries*, that in the index to *Familiar Letters of Sir*

Walter Scott (1894) there are three refer-ences under Lady Charlotte Campbell, one of which is to a Lady C——, really in-tended for the notorious Lady Conyngham, mistress to George IV. In another index Mary Bellenden is described thus : " Bellenden, Miss, Mistress of George II." This is really too bad ; for the charming maid of honour called by Gay "Smiling Mary, soft and fair as down," turned a deaf ear to the importunities of the king, as we know on the authority of Horace Walpole.

The index to Lord Braybrooke's edition of Pepys's *Diary* has many faults, mostly due to bad arrangement; but it must be allowed that there is a great difficulty in indexing a private diary such as this. The diarist knew to whom he was referring when he mentioned Mr. or Mrs.——; but where there are two or more persons of the same name, it is hard to distinguish between them correctly. This has been a stumbling-block in the compilation of the index to the new edition, in which a better system was attempted.

It has been said that a bad index is better than no index at all, but this statement is open to question. Still, all must agree that an indexless book is a great evil. Mr. J. H. Markland is the authority for the declaration that "the omission of an index when essential should be an indictable offence." Carlyle denounces the publishers of books unprovided with this necessary appendage ; and Baynes, the author of the *Archæological Epistle to Dean Mills* (usually attributed to Mason), concocted a terrible curse against such evil-doers. The reporter was the learned Francis Douce, who said to Mr. Thoms : "Sir, my friend John Baynes used to say that the man who published a book without an index ought to be damned ten miles beyond Hell, where the Devil could not get for stinging-nettles." * Lord Campbell proposed that any author who published a book without an index should be deprived of the benefits of the Copyright Act ; and the Hon. Horace Binney, LL.D., a distinguished American lawyer, held the same views, and would

* *Notes and Queries*, 5th Series, VIII. 87.

have condemned the culprit to the same punishment. Those, however, who hold the soundest views sometimes fail in practice; thus Lord Campbell had to acknowledge that he had himself sinned before the year 1857.

These are the words written by Lord Campbell in the preface to the first volume of his *Lives of the Chief Justices* (1857): "I have only further to express my satisfaction in thinking that a heavy weight is now to be removed from my conscience. So essential did I consider an index to be to every book, that I proposed to bring a Bill into Parliament to deprive an author who publishes a book without an Index of the privilege of copyright; and moreover to subject him for his offence to a pecuniary penalty. Yet from difficulties started by my printers, my own books have hitherto been without an Index. But I am happy to announce that a learned friend at the Bar, on whose accuracy I can place entire reliance, has kindly prepared a copious index, which will be appended to this work, and another for a new stereotyped edition of the Lives of the Chancellors."

Mr. John Morley, in an article in the *Fortnightly Review* on Mr. Russell's edition of Matthew Arnold's *Letters*, lifts up his voice against an indexless book. He says: " One damning sin of omission Mr. Russell has indeed perpetrated : the two volumes have no index, nor even a table of contents." * *George Selwyn and his Contemporaries*, a most interesting but badly arranged book, by John Heneage Jesse, was published without an index, and a new edition was issued (1882) also without this necessary addition. The student of the manners of the eighteenth century must constantly refer to this book, and yet it is almost impossible to find in it what you want without great waste of labour. I have found it necessary to make a manuscript index for my own use.

* Quoted *Notes and Queries*, 8th Series, IX. 425.

CHAPTER IV.

THE GOOD INDEXER.

"Thomas Norton was appointed Remembrancer of the city of London in 1570, and directions were given to him that 'he shall gather together and reduce the same [the Bookes] into Indices, Tables or Kalendars, whereby they may be more easily, readily and orderly founde.'"—*Analytical Index to " Remembrancia,"* p. v.

HE acrostic

I	I
N	never
D	did
E	ensure
X	exactness

made by a contributor to *Notes and Queries* as a motto for an index expresses very well the difficulties ever present to the indexer ; and the most successful will confess the truth that it contains,

however much others may consider his
work to be good.

There are many indexes which are only
of partial merit, but which a little more
care and experience on the part of the
indexer would have made good. If the
medium indexer felt that indexing was work
that must be done to the best of his ability, and he studied the best examples, he
would gradually become a good indexer.

The famous bibliographer, William
Oldys, rated the labours of the diligent
indexer very highly, and expressed his
views very clearly thus :

"The labour and patience, the judgment and penetration which are required
to make a good index is only known
to those who have gone through this
most painful, but least praised part of
a publication.   But laborious as it
is, I think it is indispensably necessary
to manifest the treasures of any multi-
farious collection, facilitate the knowledge
to those who seek it, and invite them to
make application thereof." *

Similar sentiments were expressed by

* *Notes and Queries,* 2nd Series, XI. 309.

a writer in the *Monthly Review* which have been quoted by Dr. Allibone in his valuable *Dictionary of English Literature.**

" The compilation of an index is one of those useful labours for which the public, commonly better pleased with entertainment than with real service, are rarely so forward to express their gratitude as we think they ought to be. It has been considered a task fit only for the plodding and the dull : but with more truth it may be said that this is the judgment of the idle and the shallow. The value of anything, it has been observed, is best known by the want of it. Agreeably to this idea, we, who have often experienced great inconveniences from the want of indices, entertain the highest sense of their worth and importance. We know that in the construction of a good index, there is far more scope for the exercise of judgment and abilities, than is commonly supposed. We feel the merits of the compiler of such an index, and we are ever ready to testify our thankfulness for his exertions."

* Vol. i., p. 85.

A goodly roll may be drawn up of
eminent men who have not been ashamed
to appear before the world as indexers.
In the first rank we must place the
younger Scaliger, who devoted ten months
on the compilation of an elaborate index
to Gruter's *Thesaurus Inscriptionum.*
Bibliographers have been unanimous in
praise of the energy exhibited by the
great critic in undertaking so vast a labour.
Antonio describes the index as a Herculean
work, and LeClerc observes that if we
think it surprising that so great a man
should undertake so laborious a task
we must remember that such indexes
can only be made by a very able man.

Nicolas Antonio, the compiler of one
of the fullest and most accurate bibliographies ever planned, was a connoisseur
of indexes, and wrote a short essay on
the makers of them.   His *Bibliotheca
Hispana* is not known so well as it
deserves to be, but those who use it find
it one of the most trustworthy of guides.
The system upon which the authors'
names are arranged is one that at first
sight may seem to give cause for ridicule,

for they appear in an alphabet of
Christian names ; but when we consider
that the Spaniards and Portuguese stand
alone among European nations in respect
to the importance they pay to the
Christian name, and remember, further,
that authors and others are often alluded
to by their Christian names alone, we
shall see a valid reason for the plan.
Another point that should not be forgotten
is the number of Spanish authors who
have belonged to the religious orders
and are never known by their surnames.
This arrangement, however, necessitates a
full index of surnames, and Antonio has
given one which was highly praised both
by Baillet and Bayle, two men who were
well able to form an opinion.

Juan de Pineda's *Monarchia Eccle-
siastica o historia Universal del Mundo*
(*Salamanca,* 1588) has a very curious and
valuable table which forms the fifth volume
of the whole set; and the three folio
volumes of indexes in one alphabet to
the *Annales Ecclesiastici* of Baronius form
a noble work.

Samuel Jeake, senior, compiled a

valuable work on "Arithmetick" in 1674, which was published by his son in 1696 : Λογιστικηλογια; or, *Arithmetick Sur- veighed and Reviewed.* Professor De Morgan specially refers to this book in his *Arithmetical Books,* saying : " Those who know the value of a large book with a good index will pick this one up when they can." He praises it on account of the value of the information it contains and the fulness of the references to that information. The alphabetical table, directing to some special points noted in the precedent treatise, was probably the work of Samuel Jeake, junior. The author's epistle is dated from Rye, 1674, and one of the entries is curious :

" Winchelsea, when drowned 74."

S. Jeake being a resident at Rye had an interesting note to add to this :

" Among the records of this town of Rye is a Memorandum entered that the year old Winchelsea was drowned (1287) corn was 2*s.* the quarter."

Thomas Carlyle denounced the putters forth of indexless books, and his sincerity is proved by the publication in 1874 of a separate index to the people's edition of his Works. In his introduction to *Cromwell's Letters and Speeches* he is very severe on some of the old folios he was forced to use :

"The Rushworths, Whitelocks, Nalsons, Thurloes; enormous folios, these and many other have been printed and some of them again printed but never yet edited, —edited as you edit wagon-loads of broken bricks, and dry mortar simply by tumbling up the wagon ! Not one of those monstrous old volumes has so much as an index. It is the general rule of editing on this matter. If your editor correct the press, it is an honourable distinction."

A very eminent name may be added to the list of indexers, for, when a boy of fifteen, Macaulay made the index to a volume of the *Christian Observer* (of which periodical his father was editor), and this he introduced to the notice of Hannah More in these words :

"To add to the list, my dear Madam, you will soon see a work of mine in print. Do not be frightened ; it is only the Index to the thirteenth volume of the *Christian Observer*, which I have had the honour of composing. Index-making, though the lowest, is not the most useless round in the ladder of literature ; and I pride myself upon being able to say that there are many readers of the *Christian Observer* who could do without Walter Scott's works, but not without those of, my dear Madam, your affectionate friend, THOMAS B. MACAULAY."

Although proud of his work, Macaulay places index-making in a very low position. In later life he used a contemptuous expression when he was describing the appearance of those who followed the lowest grade in the literary profession. The late Mr. H. Campkin, a veteran indexer, quotes this description in the preface to one of his valuable indexes— that to the twenty-five volumes of the *Sussex Archæological Collections* :

"The compilation of Indexes will always and naturally so, be regarded as a humble art ; 'index-makers in ragged coats of frieze' are classed by Lord Macaulay as the very lowest of the frequenters of the

coffee houses of the Dryden and Swift
era. Yet ''tis my vocation, Hal,' and
into very pleasant companionship it has
sometimes brought me, and if in this
probably the last of my twenty-five years'
labours in this direction, I have succeeded
in furnishing a fairly practicable key to
a valuable set of volumes, my frieze coat,
how tattered soever signifieth not, will
continue to hang upon my shoulders
not uncomfortably."

Though he did not rate highly the
calling of the indexer, Macaulay knew that
that lowly mortal has a considerable power
in his hand if he chooses to use it, for
he can state in a few words what the
author may have hidden in verbiage, and
he can so arrange his materials as to turn
an author's own words against himself.
Hence Macaulay wrote to his publishers,
" Let no d—— Tory make the index
to my History." When the index was
in progress he appears to have seen
the draught, which was fuller than he
thought necessary. He therefore wrote
to Messrs. Longmans :

" I am very unwilling to seem captious

about such a work as an Index. By all
means let Mr. —— go on. But offer him
with all delicacy and courtesy, from me
this suggestion. I would advise him to
have very few heads, except proper names.
A few there must be, such as Convoca-
tion, Nonjurors, Bank of England,
National Debt. These are heads to
which readers who wish for information
on these subject will naturally turn. But
I think that Mr.—— will on consideration
perceive that such heads as Priestcraft,
Priesthood, Party spirit, Insurrection,
War, Bible, Crown, Controversies, Dissent, are quite useless. Nobody will ever
look for them ; and if every passage in
which party-spirit, dissent, the art of war,
and the power of the Crown are mentioned, is to be noticed in the Index, the
size of the volumes will be doubled. The
best rule is to keep close to proper
names, and never to deviate from that
rule without some special occasion." *

These remarks exhibit Macaulay's
eminently common-sense view of the

* Trevelyan's *Life and Letters of Macaulay,*
chap. xi.

value of an index, but it is evident that he did not realise the possibility of a good and full index such as might have been produced. The *History of England*, with all its wealth of picturesque illustration, deserves a full index compiled by some one capable of exhibiting the spirit of that great work in a brilliant analysis.

Sir George Trevelyan's delightful *Life* of his uncle was originally published without an index, and Mr. Perceval Clark made an admirable one, both full and interesting, which was issued by the Index Society in 1881. Mr. Clark writes in his preface :

" The single heading MACAULAY of course takes up a large space of the Index, and will be found, together with a few other headings, to contain everything directly touching him. The list of his published writings refers of course only to writings mentioned by his Biographer, and lays no claim to be considered an exhaustive bibliography of his works. The books Macaulay read that were 'mostly trash' have their

places in the body of the Index, while
those that stood by him in all vicissitudes
as comforters, nurses, and companions,
have half a page to themselves under
one of the sections of MACAULAY. The
particulars of his life and work in India
are given under INDIA; localities in
London under LONDON; various newspapers under NEWSPAPERS, and certain
French and Italian towns visited by
Macaulay under their countries respectively."

Just such an index one would like to
see of the *History of England.*

It may be added that the popular
edition of the *Life* published subsequently
has an index.

A large number of official indexes
are excellent, although some very bad
ones have been printed. Still, it may
be generally stated that in Government
Departments there are those in power
who know the value of a good digest, and
understand that it is necessary to employ
skilled labour. The work is well paid,
and therefore not scamped ; and plenty of
room is devoted to the index , which is

printed in a satisfactory manner in type
well set out.

We have no modern statistics to offer,
but the often quoted statement that in
1778 a total of £12,000 was voted for
indexes to the Journals of the House of
Commons shows that the value of indexes
was appreciated by Parliament in the
eighteenth century. The items of this
amount were:

"To Mr. Edward Moore £6400 as a
final compensation for thirteen years
labour; Rev. Mr. Forster £3000 for nine
years' labour; Rev. Dr. Roger Flaxman
£3000 for nine years' labour; and £500
to Mr.Cunningham."

One of the most admirable applications
of index making is to be found in the
series of Calendars of State Papers issued
under the sanction of the Master of the
Rolls, which have made available to all
a mass of historical material of unrivalled
value. How many students have been
grateful for the indexes to these calendars,
and also for the aid given to him by the
indexes to Parliamentary papers and other
Government publications !

7

It is impossible to mention all the
good official indexes, but a special word
of praise must be given to the indexes to
the *Statutes of the Realm,* the folio edition
published by the Record Commission.
I have often consulted the *Alphabetical
Index to the Statutes from Magna Charta
to the End of the Reign of Queen Anne*
(1824) with the greatest pleasure and
profit. It is a model of good workman-
ship.

The lawyers have analytical minds, and
they know how important full indexes
and digests are to complete their stock-
in-trade. They have done much, but
there is still much to be done. Lord
Thring drew up some masterly instructions for an index to the Statute Law,
which is to be considered as a step
towards a code. These instructions
conclude with these weighty words :

" Let no man imagine that the construction of an index to the Statute Law is
a mere piece of mechanical drudgery,
unworthy of the energy and ability of an
accomplished lawyer. Next to codification, the most difficult task that can be

accomplished is to prepare a detailed plan for a code, as distinct from the easy task of devising a theoretical system of codification. Now the preparation of an index, such as has been suggested in the above instructions, is the preparation of a detailed plan for a code. Each effective title, is in effect, a plan for the codification of the legal subject-matter grouped under that title, and the whole index if completed would be a summary of a code arranged in alphabetical order." *

That this question of digesting the law is to be considered as one which should interest all classes of Englishmen, and not the lawyer only, may be seen from an article in the *Nineteenth Century* (September, 1877) on the " Improvement of the Law by Private Enterprise," by the late Sir James Fitzjames Stephen, who did so much towards a complete digest of the law. He wrote :

"I have long believed that the law might by proper means be relieved of this

* These instructions, with specimens of the proposed index, are printed in the *Law Magazine* for August, 1877, 4th Series, vol. 8, p. 491.

extreme obscurity and intricacy, and might
be displayed in its true light as a subject
of study of the deepest possible interest,
not only to every one who takes an
interest in politics or ethics, or in the
application of logic and metaphysics to
those subjects.   In short, I think that
nothing but the rearrangement and con-
densation of the vast masses of matter
contained in our law libraries is required,
in order to add to human knowledge
what would be practically a new depart-
ment of the highest and most permanent
interest.   Law holds in suspension both
the logic and the ethics, which are in
fact recognised by men of business and
men of the world as the standards by
which the practice of common life ought
to be regulated, and by which men ought
to form their opinions in all their most
important temporal affairs.   It would be
a far greater service to mankind than
many people would suppose to have
these standards clearly defined and
brought within the reach of every one
who cared to study them."
    The following remarks will apply with

equal force to a more general and universal index than that of the law :

" The preparation of a digest either of the whole or of any branch of the law is work of a very peculiar kind. It is one of the few literary undertakings in which a number of persons can really and effectively work together. Any given subject may, it is true, be dealt with in a variety of different ways ; but when the general scheme, according to which it is to be treated, has been determined on, when the skeleton of the book has been drawn out, plenty of persons might be found to do the work of filling up the details, though that work is very far from being easy or matter of routine."

The value of analytical or index work is set in a very strong light by an observation of Sir James Stephen respecting the early digesters of the law. The origin of English law is to be found in the year books and other series of old reports, which from the language used in them and the black-letter printing with its contractions, etc., are practically inaccessible. Lord Chief Justice Coke

and others who reduced these books
into form are in consequence treated as
ultimate authorities, although the almost
worshipped Coke is said by Sir James
to be "one of the most confused,
pedantic, and inaccurate of men."

A good index is that to the Works
of Jeremy Bentham, published in 1843
under the dictation of Sir John Bowring.
*The Analytical Index to the Works of
Jeremy Bentham and to the Memoirs
and Correspondence* was compiled by
J. H. Burton, to whom it does great
credit. The indexer prefixed a sensible
note, where he writes :

"In some instances it would have
been impossible to convey a notion of
the train of reasoning followed by the
author, without using his own words, and
in these no attempt has been made
to do more than indicate the place
where the subject is discussed. In other
cases where it has appeared to the compiler that an intelligible analysis has been
made, he may have failed in his necessarily abbreviated sentences in embodying
the meaning of the original, but defects

of this description are indigenous to
Indexes in general."

But here all is utility, and it is to
the literary index that we turn for
pleasure as well as instruction.

The index to Ruskin's *Fors Clavigera*,
vols. 1–8 (1887), is a most interesting book,
especially to Ruskin admirers. There
are some specially delightful original and
characteristic references under the heading
of *London*, such as the following :

" London, Fifty square miles outside of,
demoralised by upper classes

——Its middle classes compare un-
favourably with apes

——Some blue sky in, still

——Hospital named after Christ's
native village in,

——Honestest journal of, *Punch.*

——crossings, what would they be
without benevolent police ? "

The index is well made and the
references are full of life and charm,
but the whole is spoilt by the bad
arrangement. The entries are set out in
single lines under the headings in the
successive order of the pages. This looks

unsystematic, as they ought to be arranged in alphabet. When the references are given in the order of the pages they should be printed in block.

There are several entries commencing with " 's " ; thus, under

"St. George."

p. 386 :

" 's war

" of Hanover Square."

p. 387 :

" 's Square

's, Hanover Square "

p. 389 :

" 's law

's school

's message

's Chapel at Venice."

In long headings that occupy separate pages these are repeated at the top of the page, but the headings are not sufficiently full : thus the saints are arranged in alphabet under *S*; George commences on page 386. On

p. 387:

" Saint—Saints *continued*

story of,"

p. 388:

    " what of gold etc. he thinks good for
        people, they shall have "

p. 389:

    " tenth part of fortunes for "

p. 390:

    " his creed "

p. 391 :

    " loss of a good girl for his work "

In the case of all the references on
these pages you have to go back to
page 386 to find out to whom they
refer.

There is a particularly bad block of
references filling half a page under
Lord.

    " Lord, High Chancellor, 7.6 ; 's Prayer
        vital to a nation, 7.22 ; Mayor and
        Corporation, &c
    of Hosts."

It is a pity that an interesting index
should be thus marred by bad arrangement.

Dr. Birkbeck Hill's complete index to
his admirable edition of Boswell's *Life
of Johnson* is a delightful companion
to the work, and may be considered as
a model of what an index should be ;

for compilation, arrangement, and printing all are good. Under the different headings are capital abstracts in blocks. There are sub-headings in alphabet under the main heading *Johnson*.

A charming appendix to the index consists of "Dicta Philosophi: A Concordance of Johnson's Sayings."

Dr. Hill writes in his preface:

"In my Index, which has cost me many months' heavy work, 'while I bore burdens with dull patience and beat the track of the alphabet with sluggish resolution,' I have, I hope, shown that I am not unmindful of all that I owe to men of letters. To the dead we cannot pay the debt of gratitude that is their due. Some relief is obtained from its burthen, if we in our turn make the men of our own generation debtors to us. The plan on which my Index is made, will I trust be found convenient. By the alphabetical arrangement in the separate entries of each article the reader, I venture to think, will be greatly facilitated in his researches. Certain subjects I have thought it best to form into groups.

Under America, France, Ireland, London, Oxford, Paris and Scotland, are gathered together almost all the references to those subjects. The provincial towns of France, however, by some mistake I did not include in the general article. One important but intentional omission I must justify. In the case of the quotations in which my notes abound I have not thought it needful in the Index to refer to the book unless the eminence of the author required a separate and a second entry. My labour would have been increased beyond all endurance and my Index have been swollen almost into a monstrosity had I always referred to the book as well as to the matter which was contained in the passage that I extracted. Though in such a variety of subjects there must be many omissions, yet I shall be greatly disappointed if actual errors are discovered. Every entry I have made myself, and every entry I have verified in the proof sheets, not by comparing it with my manuscript, but by turning to the reference in the printed volumes. Some indulgence nevertheless may well be claimed and granted. If Homer at times nods, an index maker may be pardoned, should he in the fourth or fifth month of his task at the end of a day of eight hours' work grow drowsy. May I fondly hope that to the maker of so large an index will be extended the gratitude which Lord Bolingbroke says was once shown to lexicographers? 'I approve,' writes his lordship, 'the devotion of a studious man at Christ Church, who was overheard in his oratory entering into a detail with God, and acknowledging the divine goodness in furnishing the world with makers of dictionaries.' "

It is impossible to speak too highly of Dr. Hill's indexes to Boswell's *Life of Johnson* and Boswell's *Letters* and *Johnson Miscellanies.* Not only are they good indexes in themselves, but an indescribable literary air breathes over every page, and gives distinction to the whole. The index volume of the *Life* is by no means the least interesting of the set, and one instinctively thinks of the once celebrated Spaniard quoted by the great bibliographer Antonio—that the index of a book should be made by the author, even if the book itself were written by some one else.

The very excellence of this index has been used as a cause of complaint against its compiler. It has been said that everything that is known of Johnson can be found in the index, and therefore that the man who uses it is able to pose as a student, appearing to know as much as he who knows his *Boswell* by heart; but this is somewhat of a joke, for no useful information can be gained unless the book to which the index refers is searched, and he who honestly searches ceases to be a smatterer. It is absurd to deprive earnest readers of a useful help lest reviewers and smatterers misuse it.

Boswell himself made the original index to the *Life of Johnson*, which has several characteristic signs of its origin. Mr. Percy Fitzgerald, in his edition (1874), reprints the original "Table of Contents to the Life of Johnson," with this note:

"This is Mr. Boswell's own Index, the paging being altered to suit the present edition; and the reader will see that it bears signs of having been prepared by Mr. Boswell himself. In the second edition he made various additions, as well as alterations, which are characteristic in their way. Thus, 'Lord Bute' is changed into 'the Earl of Bute,' and 'Francis Barber' into 'Mr. Francis Barber.' After Mrs. Macaulay's name he added, 'Johnson's acute and unanswerable refutation of her levelling reveries'; and after that of Hawkins he put 'contradicted and corrected.' There are also various little compliments introduced where previously he had merely given the name. Such as 'Temple, Mr., the author's old and most intimate friend'; 'Vilette, Reverend Mr., his just claims on the publick'; Smith, Captain, his attention to Johnson at Warley Camp'; 'Somerville, Mr., the authour's warm and grateful remembrance of him'; 'Hall, General, his politeness to Johnson at Warley Camp'; Heberden, Dr., his kind attendance on Johnson.' On the

other hand, Lord Eliot's 'politeness to
Johnson' which stands in the first
edition, is cut down in the second to
the bald 'Eliot, Lord'; while 'Lough-
borough, Lord, his talents and great good
fortune,' may have seemed a little offen-
sive, and was expunged. The Literary
Club was reverentially put in capitals.
There are also such odd entries as
'Brutus, a ruffian,' &c."

One wishes that there were more indexes
like Dr. Hill's in the world; and since I
made an index to Shelley's works, I have
often thought that a series of indexes of
great authors would be of inestimable
value.

First, all the author's works should be
indexed, then his biographies, and lastly
the anecdotes and notices in reviews
and other books. How valuable would
such books be in the study of our
greatest poets! The plan is quite possible of attainment, and the indexes
would be entertaining in themselves if
made fairly full.

It is not possible to refer to all the
good indexes that have been produced,

for they are too numerous. A very
remarkable index is that of the publications of the Parker Society by Henry
Gough, which contains a great mass of
valuable information presented in a handy
form. It it the only volume issued by
the society which is sought after, as
the books themselves are a drug in the
market. Mr. Gough was employed to
make an index to the publications of
the Camden Society, which would have
been of still more value on account of
the much greater interest of the books
indexed ; but the expense of printing the
index was too great for the funds of the
society, and it had to be abandoned,
to the great loss of the literary world.
Most of the archæological societies,
commencing with the Society of Anti-
quaries, have issued excellent indexes, and
the scientific societies also have produced
indexes of varying merit.

The esteem in which the indexes of
Notes and Queries are held is evidenced
by the high prices they realise when they
occur for sale. Mr. Tedder's full indexes
to the Reports of the Conference of

Librarians and the Library Association may also be mentioned.

A very striking instance of the great value which a general index of a book may possess as a distinct work can be seen in the " Index to the first ten volumes of Book Prices Current (1887–1896), constituting a reference list of subjects and incidentally a key to Anonymous and Pseudonymous Literature, London, 1901."

Here, in one alphabet, is a brief bibliography of the books sold in ten years well set out, and the dates of the distinctive editions clearly indicated. The compilation of this index must have been a specially laborious work, and does great credit to William Jaggard, of Liverpool, the compiler.

The authorities of the Clarendon Press, Oxford, are to be highly commended for their conduct in respect to the index to Ranke's *History of England.* This was attached to the sixth volume of the work published in 1875. It is by no means a bad index in itself; but a revised index was issued in 1897, which is a

greatly improved edition by the addition
of dates and fuller descriptions and
Christian names and titles to the persons
mentioned. The new index is substanti-
ally the same as the old one, but the
reviser has gone carefully through it,
improving it at all points, by which means
it was extended over an additional twenty-
three pages. It is instructive to compare
the two editions. Four references as
they appear in the two will show the
improvement :

Old index.	*New index.*
"Lower House."	"Lower House see Commons, House of."
"Window tax v. 102."	"Window tax, imposed 1695 v. 102."
"Witt, John de."	"Witt, Cornelius de."
"Witt, Cornelius de."	"Witt, John de."

Miss Hetherington has very justly
explained the cause of bad indexing.
She says that it has been stated in the
Review of Reviews that the indexer is
born, *not* made, and that the present
writer said : " An ideal indexer needs
many qualifications ; but unlike the poet

he is not born, *but* made!" She then
adds to these differing opinions : "More
truly he is born *and* made."

I agree to the correction and forswear
my former heresy. Certainly the indexer
requires to be born with some of the
necessary qualities innate in him, and
then he requires to have those qualities
turned to a practical point by the study
of good examples, so as to know what
to follow and what to avoid. Miss
Hetherington goes on to say :

"As a matter of fact, people without
the first necessary qualifications, or any
aptitude whatever for the work are set
to compile indexes, and the work is
regarded as nothing more than purely
mechanical copying that any hack may
do. So long as indexing and cataloguing
are treated with contempt rather than
as arts not to be acquired in a day, or
perhaps a year, and so long as authors
and their readers are indifferent to good
work, wil worthless indexing continue." *

What, then, are the chief characteristics

* *Index to the Periodical Literature of the World* (1892).

that are required to form a good indexer ?
I· think they may be stated under five
headings :

1. Common-sense.
2. Insight into the meaning of the author.
3. Power of analysis.
4. Common feeling with the consulter
and insight into his mind, so that the
indexer may put the references he has
drawn from the book under headings
where they are most likely to be sought.
5. General knowledge, with the power
of overcoming difficulties.

The ignorant man cannot make a good
index. The indexer will find that his
miscellaneous knowledge is sure to come
in useful, and that which he might doubt
would ever be used by him will be found
to be helpful when least expected. It
may seem absurd to make out that the
good indexer should be a sort of Admirable Crichton. There can be no doubt,
however, that he requires a certain
amount of knowledge ; and the good
cataloguer and indexer, without knowing
everything, will be found to possess a
keen sense of knowledge.

As I owe all my interest in bibliography and indexing to him, I may perhaps be allowed to introduce the name of my elder brother, the late Mr. B. R. Wheatley, a Vice-President of the Library Association, as that of a good indexer. He devoted his best efforts to the advancement of bibliography. When fresh from school he commenced his career by making the catalogue of one of the parts of the great *Heber Catalogue.* He planned and made one of the earliest of indexes to a library catalogue—that of the Athenæum Club. He made one of the best of indexes to the transactions of a society in that of the Statistical Society, which he followed by indexes of the Transactions of the Royal Medical and Chirurgical Society, Clinical, and other societies. He also made an admirable index to Tooke's *History of Prices*—a work of great labour, which met with the high approval of the authors, Thomas Tooke and William Newmarch.

CHAPTER V.

DIFFERENT CLASSES OF INDEXES.

"Of all your talents you are a most amazing
man at Indexes. What a flag too, do you hang
out at the stern! You must certainly persuade
people that the book overflows with matter,
which (to speak the truth) is but thinly spread.
But I know all this is fair in t ade, and you have
a right to expect that the publick should purchase
freely when you reduce the whole book into an
epitome for their benefit ; I shall read the index
with pleasure."—WILLIAM CLARKE TO WILLIAM
BOWYER, NICHOLS'S *Literary Anecdotes*, vol. 3,
p. 46.

IN dealing with the art of the
indexer it is most important to
consider the different classes of
indexes. There are simple indexes, such as those of names and
places, which only require care and
proper alphabetical arrangement. The

makers of these often plume themselves upon their work ; but they must
remember that the making of these indexes can only be ranked as belonging
to the lowest rung of the index ladder.

The easiest books to index are those
coming within the classes of History,
Travel, Topography, and generally those
that deal almost entirely with facts. The
indexing of these is largely a mechanical
operation, and only requires care and
judgment. Verbal indexes and concordances are fairly easy when the plan
is settled ; but they are often works of
great labour, and the compilers deserve
great credit for their perseverance. John
Marbeck stands at the head of this body
of indefatigable workers who have placed
the world under the greatest obligations.
He was the first to publish a concordance
of the Bible,* to be followed nearly two
centuries later by the work of Alexander

---

* " A Concordance, that is to saie, a worke
wherein by the ordre of the letters of the ABC
ye maie redely finde any worde conteigned in
the whole Bible, so often as it is there expressed
or mencioned . . . anno 1550."—*Folio.*

Cruden, whose name has almost become a synonym for a concordance. After the Bible come the works of Shakespeare, indexed by Samuel Ayscough (1790), Francis Twiss (1805), Mrs. Cowden Clarke (1845), and Mr. John Bartlett, who published in 1894 a still fuller concordance than that of Mrs. Clarke. It is a vast quarto volume of 1,910 pages in double columns, and represents an enormous amount of self-denying labour. Dr. Alexander Schmidt's *Shakespeare Lexicon* (1874) is something more than a concordance, for it is a dictionary as well.

A dictionary is an index of words. We do not mention dictionaries in this connection to insist on the fact that they are indexes of words, but rather to point out that a dictionary such as those of Liddell and Scott, Littré, Murray, and Bradley, reaches the high watermark of index work, and so the ordinary indexer is able to claim that he belongs to the same class as the producers of such masterpieces as these.

Scientific books are the most difficult to index; but here there is a difference between the science of fact and the science of thought, the latter being the most difficult to deal with. The indexing of books of logic and ethics will call forth all the powers of the indexer and show his capabilities; but what we call the science of fact contains opinions as well as facts, and some branches of political economy are subjects by no means easy to index.

Some authors indicate their line of reasoning by the compilation of headings. This is a great help to the indexer; but if the author does not present such headings, the indexer has to make them himself, and he therefore needs the abilities of the *précis*-writer.

There are indexes of Books, of Transactions, Periodicals, etc., and indexes of Catalogues. Each of these classes demands a different method. A book must be thoroughly indexed; but the index of Journals and Transactions may be confined to the titles of the papers and articles. It is, however, better to index the contents of the essays as well as their titles.

Before the indexer commences his work he must consider whether his index is to be full or short. Sometimes it is not necessary to adopt the full index— frequently it is too expensive a luxury for publisher or author ; but the short index can be done well if necessary.

Whatever plan is followed, the indexer must use his judgment. This ought to be the marked characteristic of the good indexer. The bad indexer is entirely without this great gift.

While trying to be complete, the indexer must reject the trivial ; and this is not always easy. He must not follow in the steps of the lady who confessed that she only indexed those points which specially interested her. We have fair warning of incompleteness in *The Register of Corpus Christi Guild, York*, published by the Surtees Society in 1872, where we read, on page 321 :

" This Index contains the names of all persons mentioned in the appendix and foot-notes, but a selection only is given of those who were admitted into the Guild or enrolled in the Obituary."

The plan here adopted is not to be commended, for it is clear that so important a name-list as this is should be thoroughly indexed. However learned and judicious an editor may be, we do not choose to submit to his judgment in the offhand decision of what is and what is not important.

There is a considerable difference in the choice of headings for a general or special index—say, for instance, in indexing electrical subjects the headings would differ greatly in the indexes of the Institution of Civil Engineers or of the Institution of Electrical Engineers. In the former, dynamos, transformers, secondary or storage batteries, alternate and continuous currents would probably be grouped under the general heading of Electricity, while in the latter we shall find Dynamos under D, Transformers under T, Batteries under B, Alternate under A, and Continuous under C.

The indexes to catalogues of libraries, etc., are among the most difficult of indexes to compile. It was not usual to attach an index of subjects to a catalogue of authors until late years, and that to the *Catalogue of the Athenæum Club Library* (1851) is an early specimen. The *New York State Library Catalogue* (1856) has an index, as have those of the *Royal Medical and Chirurgical Society* (1860) and the *London Library* (1865 and 1875). That appended to the *Catalogue of the Manchester Free Library* (1864) is more a short list of titles than an index.

There are special difficulties attendant on the indexing of catalogues. Books are written in many languages, and there is considerable trouble in bringing together the books on a given subject produced in many countries. The titles of books are not drawn up on the same system or with any wish to help the indexer. Titles are seldom straightforward, for they are largely concocted to attract the readers, without any honest wish to express correctly the nature of the contents of the book. They are usually either too short or too enigmatical. The titles of pamphlets, again, are often too long; and it may be taken as an axiom that the longer the title the less important the book.

The indexer, however, has a great advantage over the cataloguer, because the latter is bound by bibliographical etiquette not to alter the title of a book, while the indexer is at liberty to alter the title as he likes, so as to bring together books on the same subject, however different the titles may be. Herein consists the great objection to the index composed of short titles, as in Dr. Crestadoro's *Index to the Manchester Free Library Catalogue.* Books almost entirely alike in subject are separated by reason of the different wording of the titles. It is much more convenient to gather together under one entry books identical in subject, and there is no utility in separating an "elementary treatise" on electricity from "the elements" of electricity. One important point connected with indexes to catalogues is to add the date of the book after the name of the author, so that the seeker may know whether the book is old or new.

An index ought not to supersede the table of contents, as this is often useful for those who cannot find what they want in the index, from having forgotten the point of the heading under which it would most likely appear in the alphabet.

In the year 1900 there was a controversy in *The Times* on a proposed subject index to the catalogue of the library of the British Museum. It was commenced on October 15th by a letter signed " A Scholar," and closed on November 19th by the same writer, who summed up the whole controversy. " A Scholar" expressed himself strongly against the proposal, and as he himself confesses he used very arrogant language. In consequence of which, most readers must have desired to find him proved to be in the wrong. This desire was satisfied when Mr. Fortescue, the keeper of the printed books at the British Museum, delivered his address as President of the Library Association on August 27th last.

The two points made by the "Scholar" were: (1) That the making of a general subject index to the catalogue proposed by the authorities of the British Museum would be a waste of money; (2) That it was a great evil for the five-yearly indexes originated by Mr. Fortescue to be discontinued.

Now let us see what is to be said with authority on these points.

Mr. Fortescue said :

" Last Autumn. . . I read with respectful astonishment a letter to ' The Times ' from a writer who preferred to veil his identity under the modest signature of ' a Scholar.' There I read that ' the studious public of this country and Europe in general have been surprised by the news that the authorities of the British Museum seriously contemplate the compilation of a subject index to the vast collection of printed books in that library.' I can assure you that the surprise of the studious public and of Europe in general cannot have surpassed my own when I thus learned of what the authorities were seriously contemplating. Nevertheless, it left me able, I thought, to discern that their vast conceptions had not been so fortunate as to gain the approval of ' a Scholar ' and to marvel whence *The Times* and other great journals had drawn their truly

surprising information.   Some of the
arguments put forth in sundry criticisms
of the ' scheme ' showed how much thought
had been bestowed upon matters which
then first dazzled my bewildered imagination.   It may come some day (who shall
say what will not ?), this General Index,
or it may never come.   But up to the
present   moment   I   am   aware   of   no
authority who is seriously contemplating
so   large   a   venture   unless   perhaps   it   be
' a Scholar ' himself."

Then as to the five-yearly indexes
Mr. Fortescue said :

" Experience has taught us that there
is no form of subject-index which the
public values so highly as one which gives
the most recent literature on every possible
subject.   And to meet this manifest want
we shall certainly continue to issue, with
all the latest improvements I hope, the
modest Indexes which we have hitherto
published in five-yearly (I am afraid as
President of The Library Association I
should say ' in quinquennial ') volumes.
The Museum sweeps its net so wide and
in such remote seas that a more or less

complete collection of books on almost every subject or historical event is gathered within it for future students. To take only two incidents from the last year or two, the next index will contain not less than a hundred and forty books and pamphlets, in almost every European tongue, on the Dreyfus case, and from four to five hundred books on the present war in South Africa. Such bibliographical tests have more than an ephemeral or immediate value. They will remain as records of events or phases of thought long after their causes shall have faded from all but the page of history."

Of late years the dictionary catalogue has come very largely into use in public libraries. This consists of a union of catalogue of authors and index of subjects which is found to be very useful and illuminating to the readers in free libraries, most of whom are probably not versed in the niceties of bibliographical arrangement, but are more likely to want a book on a particular subject than to require a special book which they know. Mr. Cutter has written the history of the

dictionary catalogue in the *United States
Special Report* (pp. 533–539), and he
traces it back in America to about the
year 1815.

Excellent specimens of these dictionary
catalogues have been produced. They
are of great value to the ordinary reader
at a small public library, but I venture
to think that to construct one for a
large library is a waste of power, because
if several large libraries of a similar
character do the same thing, there is
constant repetition and considerable loss
by the unnecessary outlay. If a fairly
complete standard index were made, it
could be used by all the libraries, and
in return the libraries might unite to
pay its cost. I am pleased to know
that Mr. Fortescue prefers to keep index
and catalogue distinct. He said in his
address :

"I have formed, so far as I know,
but one dogmatic conviction, and it is
this : that the best catalogue which the
art of man can invent is a catalogue in
two inter-dependent yet independent
parts ; the first and greater part an

alphabetical catalogue of authors, the second and lesser part a subject-index. I know well that I shall be told that I am out of date, that such an opinion is as the voice of one crying in the wilderness—that the dictionary catalogue has won its battle—but even so, perhaps the more so, do I feel it the part of a serious and immovable conviction to declare my belief that—for student and librarian alike—this twofold catalogue, author and subject each in its own division, is the best catalogue a library can have, and that the dictionary catalogue is the very worst. But whatever may be our individual opinion on this head, it is only necessary to enter into a very simple calculation to see that if the dictionary system could have governed the rules of the British Museum Catalogue it would by now have consisted of not less than twelve million entries ; and assuredly it would have been neither completed nor printed to-day."

CHAPTER VI.

GENERAL RULES FOR ALPHABETICAL INDEXES.

"In order to guard against blunders Bayle proposed that certain directions should be drawn up for the guidance of the compilers of indexes."

HESE rules, originally drawn up by a committee of the Index Society, were primarily intended for the use of indexers making indexes of indexless books to be published by the society, which, being produced separately from the books themselves, needed some introductory note. In all cases, however, some explanation of the mode of compilation should be attached to the index. The compiler comes fresh from his difficulties and the expedients he has devised to overcome them, and it is therefore well for him to explain to the user of the index what those special difficulties are.

The object of the Index Society was to set up a standard of uniformity in the compilation of the indexes published by them. Although rigid uniformity is not needed in all indexes, it is well that these should be made in accordance with the best experience of past workers rather than on a system which varies with the mood of the compiler. It is hoped that the following rules may be of some practical use to future indexers.

In the eighth chapter of *How to Catalogue a Library* there are a series of rules for making a catalogue of a small library in which are codified the different points which had been discussed in the previous chapters. In the present chapter the Index Society rules are printed in italic, and to them are now added some illustrative remarks. There is necessarily a certain likeness between rules for indexing and rules for cataloguing, but the differences are perhaps more marked. At all events, the rules for one class of work will not always be suitable for the other class.

1. *Every work should have one index to the whole set, and not an index to each volume.*

An index to each volume of a set is convenient if a general amalgamated index to the whole set is given as well; but a work with several indexes and no general one is most inconvenient and irritating, while to have both seems extravagant. If, however, the author or publisher is willing to present both, it is not for the user of the book to complain.

2. *Indexes to be arranged in alphabetical order, proper names and subjects being united in one alphabet. An introduction containing some indication of the classification of the contents of the book indexed to be prefixed.*

In an alphabetical index the alphabet must be all in all. When the alphabet is used, it must be used throughout. There is no advantage in dividing proper names from subjects, as is so often done, particularly in foreign indexes, Another objectionable practice frequently adopted in the indexes of periodical publications is to keep together the entries under the separate headings used in the journal itself, and thus to have a number of distinct alphabets under different headings. This union of alphabetical and classified indexing has been condemned on a former page, and need not here be referred to further.

In the case of large headings the items should be arranged in alphabetical order under them. There is occasionally a difficulty in carrying this out completely, but it should be attempted. We want as little classification as possible in an alphabetical index. Mr. W. F. Poole wisely said in reference to the proposal of one of his helpers on the *Index of Periodical Literature* to place Wealth, Finance, and Population under the heading of Political Economy: " The fatal defect of every classified arrangement is that nobody understands it except the person who made it and he is often in doubt."

3. *The entries to be arranged according to the order of the English alphabet. I and J and U and V to be kept distinct.*

There are few things more irritating

than to find the alphabet confused by the
union of the vowel *i* with the consonant *j*,
or the vowel *u* with the consonant *v*.   No
doubt they were not distinguished some
centuries ago, but this is no reason why
they should again be confused now that
they are usually distinct.   There may
be special reasons why they should be
mixed together in the British Museum
Catalogue, but it is not evident that
these are sufficient.

The only safe rule is to use the English
alphabet as it is to-day in an English
index.   One of the rules of the American
Library Association is: " The German
ae, oe, ue always to be written *a, o, u*, and
arranged as *a, o, u*." By this Goethe
would have to be written Gothe, which is
now an unusual form, and I think it would
be better to insist that where both forms
are used, one or other should be chosen
and all instances spelt alike.   It is a
very common practice to arrange *a, o, u*,
as if they were written *ae, oe, ue* ; but
this leads to the greatest confusion, and
no notice should be taken of letters that
are merely to be understood.

4. *Headings consisting of two or more distinct words are not to be treated as integral portions of one word ; thus the arrangement should be :*

Grave, John		*Grave* at Kherson
Grave at Kherson		*Grave*, John
Grave of Hope	not	*Gravelot*
Grave Thoughts		*Grave* of Hope
Gravelot		*Gravesend*
Gravesend		*Grave* Thoughts.

The perfect alphabetical arrangement is often ignored, and it is not always easy to decide as to what is the best order ; but the above rule seems to put the matter pretty clearly. If no system is adhered to, it becomes very difficult to steer a course through the confusion. When such entries are printed, a very incongruous appearance often results from the use of a line to indicate repetition when a word similar in spelling, but not really the same word, occurs ; thus, in the above, Grave *surname*, Grave *substantive*, and Grave *adjective* must all be repeated. It is inattention to this obvious fact that

has caused such ludicrous blunders as
the following :

> "Mill on Liberty
> —— on the Floss." *
> "Cotton, Sir Willoughby,
> ——, price of."
> "Old age
> —— Artillery Yard
> —— Bailey."

These are all genuine entries taken from
books, and similar blunders are not
uncommon even in fairly good indexes;
thus, in the *Calendar of Treasury Papers,*
1714–1719, issued by the Public Record
Office, under *Ireland* are the following
entries :

"Ireland, Mrs. Jane, Sempstress and
Starcher to King William ; cxcvii. 32.

---

* Miss Hetherington gives an additional instance
of this class of blunder, but her only authority is
" said to be from the index of a young lady's scrap
book " :

> "Patti, Adelina,
> —— oyster."

The example in the text is absolutely genuine,
although it has been doubted.

. . . . Attorney General of, *See* Attorney General, Ireland."

Then follow nearly two columns on Ireland with the marks of repetition (. . .) throughout.

The names of streets in the *Post Office Directory* are now arranged in a strict alphabetical order on the lines laid down in this rule ; thus we have :

> " White Street
> White's Row
> White Heart
> Whitechapel."

Again :

> " Abbott Road
> Abbott Street
> Abbott's Road."

Again :

> " King Square
> King Street
> King and Queen Street
> King David Street
> King Edward Road
> King William Street
> King's Arms Court

King's Road
Kinglake Street
Kingsbury Road
Kingsgate Street."

Sometimes there is a slip, as might be expected in so complicated a list of names. Thus in the foregoing sequence Kinghorn Street comes between King William Street and King's Arms Court, while I think it ought to come immediately before Kinglake Street; but, after all, this is a matter of opinion. Strattondale Street comes before Stratton Street; but this is merely a case of missorting.

There is one piece of alphabetisation which the editor of the *Post Office Directory* has always adopted, and that is to place Upper and Lower under those adjectives, and Old Bond Street under *Old*, and New Bond Street under *New*. These two names belong to what is practically one street (although each division is separately numbered), which is always spoken of as Bond Street, and therefore for which the majority of persons will look under Bond. South Molton

Street is correctly placed under South because there is no North Molton Street, and the street is named after South Molton ; while South Eaton Place is merely a continuation of Eaton Place. Some persons, however, think that names should be treated as they stand, and that we should not go behind them to find out what they mean.

5. *Proper Names of foreigners to be arranged alphabetically under the prefixes—*

Dal		Dal Sie
Del		Del Rio
Della		Della Casa
Des	as	Des Cloiseaux
Du		Du Bois
La		La Condamine
Le		Le Sage,

but not under the prefixes—

D	as	Abbadie	not	D'Abbadie
Da	„	Silva	„	Da Silva
De	„	La Place	„	De La Place
Von	„	Humboldt	„	Von Humboldt
Van	„	Beneden	„	Van Beneden.

It is an acknowledged principle that when the prefix is a preposition it is to be rejected; but when an article, it is to be retained. When, however, as in the case of the French Du, Des, the two are joined, it is necessary to retain the preposition. This also applies to the case of the Italian Della, which is often rejected by cataloguers. English names are, however, to be arranged under the prefixes :

$$\left.\begin{array}{l} De \\ Dela \\ Van \end{array}\right\} \ as \ \left\{\begin{array}{l} De\ Quincey \\ Delabeche \\ Van\ Mildert, \end{array}\right.$$

because these prefixes are meaningless in English, and form an integral part of the name.

Whatever rule is adopted, some difficulty will be found in carrying it out : for instance, if we consider Van Dyck as a foreigner, his name will appear as Dyck (Van); but if as an Englishman, his name will be treated as Vandyck.

A prefix which is translated into the relative term in a foreign language cannot be considered as a fixed portion of the name. Thus Alexander von Humboldt, when away from his native Germany, translated his name into Alexandre de Humboldt. The reason why prefixes are retained in English names is because they have no meaning in themselves, and cannot be translated. There is a difficulty here in respect to certain names with De before them; for instance, the Rothschilds call themselves De Roth-schild, but when the head of the family in England was made a peer of the United Kingdom he became Lord Rothschild without the De. In fact, we have to come to the conclusion that when men think of making changes in their names they pay very little attention to the difficulties they are forging for the cataloguer and the indexer.

In this rule no mention is made of such out-of-the-way forms as Im Thurn and Ten Brink. It is very difficult to decide upon the alphabetical position of these names. If the indexer had to deal with a number of these curious prefixes, it would probably be well to ignore them ; but when in the case of an English index they rarely occur, it will probably be better to put Im Thurn under I and Ten Brink under T.

With respect to the translation of foreign titles, the historian Freeman made a curious statement which is quoted in one of the American Q.P. indexes. Freeman wrote :

"No man was ever so clear [as Macaulay] from the vice of thrusting in foreign words into an English sentence. One sees this in such small matters as the accurate way in which he uses foreign titles. He speaks, for instance, of the 'Duke of Maine,' the 'Count of Avaux,' while in other writers one sees the vulgarism of the *Court Circular*, 'Duke de Maine,' 'Duc de Maine,'—perhaps 'Duc of Maine.'"

Duke de Maine and Duc of Maine may be vulgar, they are certainly incorrect; but I fail to see how it can be vulgar to call a man by his right name —"Duc de Maine." I do not venture to censure Macaulay, but for lesser men it is certainly a great mistake to translate the names of foreigners, in spite of Freeman's expression of his strong opinion.

6. *Proper names with the prefix St.,
as St. Albans, St. John, to be arranged
in the alphabet as if written in full—Saint.
When the word Saint represents a cere-
monial title, as in the case of St. Alban,
St. Giles, and St. Augustine, these names
are to be arranged under the letters A and
G respectively; but the places St. Albans,
St. Giles's, and St. Augustine's will be
found under the prefix Saint. The prefixes
M' and Mc to be arranged as if written
in full—Mac.*

This rule is very frequently neglected,
more particularly in respect to the neglect
of the difference between Saint Alban the
man and St. Albans the place.

7. *Peers to be arranged under their
titles, by which alone in most cases they are
known, and not under their family names,
except in such a case as Horace Walpole,
who is almost unknown by his title of
Earl of Orford, which came to him late
in life. Bishops, deans, etc., to be always
under their family names.*

About this rule there is great difference
of opinion. The British Museum practice

is to catalogue peers under their surnames,
and the same plan has been adopted in the
Dictionary of National Biography.   It is
rather difficult to understand how this
practice has come into being.   There are
difficulties on both sides ; but the great
majority of peers are, I believe, known
solely by their titles, and when these
noblemen are entered under their family
names   cross   references   are   required
because very few persons know the family
names of peers.   The Library Association   and   Bodleian   rules   adopt   the
common-sense plan of entering noblemen
under their titles, and Mr. Cutter gives
some   excellent   reasons   for   doing this,
although he cannot make up his mind to
run counter to a supposed well-established
rule.   Mr. Cutter writes :

"STANHOPE Philip Dormer, 4th *Earl
of Chesterfield.* . . .   This is the British
Museum rule and Mr. Jewett's.   Mr.
Perkins prefers entry under titles for
British noblemen also, in which I should
agree with him if the opposite practice
were not so well established.   The reasons
for entry under the title are that British

noblemen are always spoken of, always sign by their titles only, and seldom put the family name upon the title-pages of their books, so that ninety-nine in a hundred readers must look under the title first. The reasons against it are that the founders of noble families are often as well known—sometimes even better— by their family name as by their titles (as Charles Jenkinson, afterwards Lord Liverpool; Sir Robert Walpole, afterwards Earl of Orford); that the same man bears different titles in different parts of his life (thus P. Stanhope published his *History of England from the Peace of Utrecht* as Lord Mahon, and his *Reign of Queen Anne* as Earl Stanhope); that it separates members of the same family (Lord Chancellor Eldon would be under Eldon, and his father and all his brothers and sisters under the family name, Scott), [Mr. Cutter forgot that Lord Eldon's elder brother William was also a peer— Lord Stowell] and brings together members of different families (thus the earldom of Bath has been held by members of the families of Chande,

Bourchier, Granville and Pulteney, and the family name of the present Marquis of Bath is Thynne), which last argument would be more to the point in planning a family history."

The advocates of the practice of arranging peers under their family names make much of the difficulties attendant on such changes of name as Francis Bacon, Viscount St. Alban's, Benjamin Disraeli (afterwards Earl of Beaconsfield), Sir John Lubbock (now Lord Avebury), and Richard Monckton Milnes (afterwards Lord Houghton). These, doubtless, are difficulties, but I believe that they amount in all to very few as compared with the cases on the other side.

This is a matter that might be settled by calculation, and it would be well worth while to settle it. Mr. Cutter says that ninety-nine in a hundred must look under the title first, but I doubt if the percentage be quite as high as this. If it were, it ought to be conclusive against any other arrangement than that under titles.

Moreover, these instances do not really

meet the case, for they belong to another class, which has to be dealt with in cataloguing—that is, those who change their names. When a man succeeds to a peerage he changes his name just as a Commoner may change his name in order to succeed to a certain property.

8. *Foreign compound names to be arranged under the first name, as Lacaze Duthiers. English compound names under the last, except in such cases as Royston-Pigott, where the first name is a true surname. The first name in a foreign compound is, as a rule, the surname ; but the first name in an English compound is usually a mere Christian name.*

This rule is open to some special difficulties. It can be followed with safety in respect to foreign names, but special knowledge is required in respect to English names. Of late years a large number of persons have taken a fancy to bring into prominence their last Christian name when it is obtained from a surname. They then hyphen their Christian name with their surname, because they wish to be called by both. The Smiths and the Joneses commenced the practice, but others have followed their lead. The indexer has no means of telling whether in a hyphened name the first name is a real surname or not, and he needs to know much personal and family history before he can decide correctly.

Hyphens are used most recklessly nowadays, and the user has no thought of the trouble he gives to the indexer. If the Christian name is hyphened to the surname, and all the family agree to use the two together as their surname, the indexer must treat the compound name as a true surname. Often a hyphen is used merely to show that the person bearing the names wishes to be known by both, but with no intention of making the Christian name into a surname. Thus a father may not give all his children the same Christian name, but change it for each individual, as one son may be James Somerset-Jones and another George Balfour-Jones. In such a case as this the hyphen is quite out of place, and

Jones must still be treated as the only surname. No one has a right to expect his Christian name to be treated as a surname merely by reason of his joining the Christian name to the surname by a hyphen. He must publicly announce his intention of treating his Christian name as a surname, or change it by Act of Parliament. Even when the name is legally changed, there is often room for confusion. The late Mr. Edward Solly, F.R.S., who was very interested in these inquiries, drew my attention to the fact that the family of Hesketh changed their name in 1806 to Bamford by Act of Parliament, and subsequently obtained another Act to change it back to Hesketh. The present form of the family names is Lloyd-Hesketh-Bamford-Hesketh.

With respect to Spanish and Portuguese names it is well to bear in mind that there are several surnames made from Christian names, as, for instance, Fernando is a Christian name and Fernandez is a surname, just as with us Richard is a Christian name and Richards a surname.

9. *An adjective is frequently to be*

preferred to a substantive as a catchword ; for instance, when it contains the point of the compound, as Alimentary Canal, English History ; also when the compound forms a distinctive name, as Soane Museum.

The object of this rule is often overlooked, and many indexers purposely reject the use of adjectives as headings. One of the most marked instances of an opposite rule may be seen in the index to Hare's *Walks in London* (1878), where all the alleys, bridges, buildings, churches, courts, houses, streets, etc., are arranged under these headings, and not under the proper name of each. There may be a certain advantage in some of these headings, but few would look for Lisson Grove under Grove, and the climax of absurdity is reached when Chalk Farm is placed under Farm.

10. *The entries to be as short as is consistent with intelligibility, but the insertion of names without specification of the cause of reference to be avoided, except in particular cases. The extent of the references, when more than one page, to be marked by indicating the first and last pages.*

This rule requires to be carried out with judgment. Few things are more annoying than a long string of references without any indication of the cause of reference, but on the other hand it is objectionable to come across a frivolous entry. The consulter is annoyed to find no additional information in the book to what is already given in the index. It will therefore be found best to set out the various entries in which some fact or opinion is mentioned, and then to gather together the remaining references under the heading of *Alluded to.*

The most extreme instances of annoying block lists of references under a name are to be found in Ayscough's elaborate index to the *Gentleman's Magazine,* where all the references under one surname are placed together without even the distinction of the Christian name. The late Mr. Edward Solly made a curious calculation as to the time that would be employed in looking up these references. For instance, under the name Smith there are 2,411 entries *en masse,* and with no initial letters. If there were these divisions, one would find Zachary Smith in a few minutes, but now one must look to each reference to find what is wanted. With taking down the volumes and hunting through long lists of names, Mr. Solly found that two minutes were occupied in looking up each reference ; hence it might take the consulter eight days (working steadily ten hours a day) to find out if there be any note about Zachary Smith in the magazine, a task which no one would care to undertake.

A like instance of bad indexing will be found in Scott's edition of Swift's *Works.* Here there are 638 references to Robert Harley, Earl of Oxford, without any indication of the reason why his name is entered in the index. This case also affords a good instance of careless indexing in another particular, for these references are separated under different headings instead of being gathered under one, as follows :

Harley (Robert)   277 references.
Oxford (Lord)   111   ,,
Treasurer, Lord Oxford 300   ,,

The late Mr. B. R. Wheatley read a paper before the Conference of Librarians (1877) on this subject of indexes, without details of the reason or cause of reference, entitled, "An 'Evitandum' in Index-making, principally met with in French and German Periodical Scientific Literature" (*Transactions*, p. 88). He pointed out that often in German Indexes the entries in the *Sach Register* would be full and correct, while those in the *Namen Register* would usually be meagre, and consist merely of the surnames of the authors and the initials of their Christian names. He then referred to many instances of the uselessness of these indexes. He further referred to the forty so-called indexes of subjects added to Allibone's valuable *Critical Dictionary of English Literature*, which are practically useless. He concluded his paper with these words :

"You are referred to the 'Morals and Manners' index for such varied subjects as Apparitions, Divorce, Marriage, Duelling, Freemasonry, Mormonism, Mythology, Spiritualism and Witchcraft. There are 1,365 names in this index, and how

are you to discover which belong to any
of the above subjects without wading
through the whole? It is, in fact, an
entire system of indexing backwards
from particulars to generals, instead of
from generals to particulars. It is something like writing on a sign-post on the
road to Bath, 'To Somersetshire,' and
if in one phrase I were to add a characteristic entry to these sub-indexes, or
to give one form of reference which
should be typical of this style of index,
I should say—Needle, *see* Bottle of Hay.
You find the bottle of hay—but where
is the needle?"

The form in which the various entries
in an index are to be drawn up is worthy
of much attention, and particular care
should be taken to expunge all redun-
dant words. For example, it would be
better to write :

"Smith (John), his character; his
  execution,"

than

"Smith (John), character of; execution of";

or

" Brown (Robert) saves money,"
than
" Brown (Robert), saving of money by."
A good instance of the frivolous entry
is the hackneyed quotation,

" Best (Mr. Justice), his great mind,"
which is supposed to be a reference to
a passage in this form : " Mr. Justice
Best said that he had a great mind to
commit the man for trial." This particular reference is almost too good to
be true, and I have not been able to
trace it to its source. That has been
said to be in the index to one of
Chitty's law-books, and it is added that
possibly Chitty had a grudge against
Sir William Draper Best, one of the
Puisne Judges of the King's Bench from
1819 to 1824, and Lord Chief Justice
of the Common Pleas from 1824 to
1829, in which latter year he was created
Lord Wynford. Another explanation is
that it was a joke of Leigh Hunt's, who
first published it in the *Examiner*.

11. *Short entries to be repeated under
such headings as are likely to be required,
in place of a too frequent use of cross*

references.   These references, however, to be made from cognate headings, as Cerebral to Brain, and vice versâ, where the subject matter is different.

Cross references are very useful, but they are not usually popular with those who are unaccustomed to them.   They ought to be used where the number of references under a certain heading is large, but it is always better to duplicate the references than to refer too often to insignificant entries.

12.   *In the case of journals and transactions brief abstracts of the contents of the several articles or papers to be drawn up and arranged in the alphabetical index under the heading of the article.*

The advantage of this plan is that a *précis* can be made of the articles or papers which will be useful to the reader as containing an abstract of the contents, much of which might not be of sufficient importance to be sorted out in the alphabet; in the case where the entries are important they can be duplicated in the alphabet. A good specimen of this plan of indexing may be found in the indexes to the Journal of the Statistical Society.

13. *Authorities quoted or referred to in a book, to be indexed under each author's name, the titles of his works being separately set out and the word " quoted" added in italics.* This rule is quite clear, and there is nothing to be added to it. It is evident that all books quoted should be indexed.

14. *When the indexed page is large, or contains long lists of names, it is to be divided into four sections, referred to respectively as a, b, c, d; thus if a page contains* 64 *lines,* 1–16 *will be a,* 17–32 *b,* 33–48 *c,* 49–64 *d. If in double columns, the page is still to be divided into four—a and b forming the upper and lower halves of the first column, and c and d the upper and lower halves of the second column.* This division of the page will often be found very useful, and save much time to the consulter.

15. *When a work is in more than one volume, the number of the volume is to be specified by small Roman numerals. In the case of long sets, such as the " Gentleman's*

Magazine," a special Arabic numeral for indicating the volume, distinct from the page numeral, may be employed with advantage.

The frequent use of high numbers in Roman capitals is very inconvenient.

16. *Entries which refer to complete chapters or distinct papers, to be printed in small capitals or italics.*

This is useful as indicating that the italic entry is of more importance than those in Roman type.

17. *Headings to be printed in a marked type. A dash, instead of indentation, to be used as a mark of repetition. The dash to be kept for entries exactly similar, and the word to be repeated when the second differs in any way from the first. The proper name to be repeated when that of a different person. In the case of joint authors, the Christian name or initials of the first, whose surname is arranged in the alphabet, to be in parentheses, but the Christian names of the second to be in the natural order, as Smith (John) and Alexander Brown, not Smith (John) and Brown (Alexander).*

Dashes should be of a uniform length, and that length should not be too great. It is a mistake to suppose that the dash is to be the length of the line which is not repeated. If it be necessary to make the repetition of a portion of the title as well as the author, this should be indicated by another dash, and not by the elongation of the former one.

The reason for the last direction in this rule is that the Christian name is only brought back in order to make the alphabetical position of the surname clear ; and as this is not necessary in respect to the second person, the names should remain in their natural order.

The initials which stand for Christian names often give much trouble, particularly among foreigners. Most Frenchmen use the letter M. to stand for monsieur, giving no Christian name ; but sometimes M. stands for Michel or other Christian name commencing with M. The Germans are often very careless in the use of initials, and I have found in one index of a scientific periodical the following specimens of this confusion :

(1) H. D. Gerling, (2) H. W. Brandes, (3) D. W. Olbers. Here all three cases look alike, but in the first H. D. represent two titles—Herr Doctor ; in the second, H. W. represent two Christian names— Heinrich Wilhelm; and in the third one title and one Christian name— Dr. W. Olbers.

The above rules do not apply to subject indexes, and in certain cases may need modification in accordance with the special character of the work to be indexed. On the whole, it may be said that an alphabetical index is the best; but under special circumstances it may be well to have a classified index. Generally it may be said that there are special objections to classification, and therefore if a classified index is decided upon, it must needs be exceptional, and rules must be made for it by the maker of the index.

In the foregoing rules no mention is made of the difficulties attendant on the use of Oriental names. Under " Rules for a Small Library " in *How to Catalogue a Library*, I wrote :

" 7. Oriental names to be registered in accordance with the system adopted by a recognised authority on the subject."

This, however, is only shifting the responsibility. In an ordinary English index this point is not likely to give much trouble, and the rule may be safely adopted of registration under the first name. But where there are many names to be dealt with, difficulties are sure to arise. In India the last name is usually adopted, and the forenames are frequently contracted into initials, so that it is obligatory to use this name. We must never forget the practical conclusion that a man's real name is that by which he is known. But the indexer's difficulty in a large number of cases is that he does not know what that name is. Sir George Birdwood has kindly drawn up for me the following memorandum on the subject, which is of great value, from the interesting historical account of the growth of surnames in India under British rule which he gives.

On the Indexing of the Names of Eastern People.

Confining myself to the people – Parsees, Hindoos, and Mussulmans (*muslimin*)—of India, I find it very difficult to state an unexceptionable rule for the indexing of their names ; and I index them in the order in which they are signed by the people themselves. The first or forename of a Parsee or a Hindoo, but not of a Mussulman if he be a Pathan, is his own personal or, as we say, " Christian "—that is, baptismal or " water "—name ; and their second their father's personal name, and not his family or, as we say, " blood " name, or true surname. The naming of individuals in the successive generations of a Parsee or Hindoo, and certain Mussulmanee families, runs thus : A. G., N. A., U. N., and so on, the grandfather's name disappearing in the third generation.

The Parsees only in comparatively recent times adopted family or true surnames derived from the personal or paternal names, or both, of the first distinguished member of the family, or from his occupation or place of residence, or from some notable friend or patron of his, or from some title conferred on him by the ruler whose subject he was. Thus the Patels of Bombay are descended from Rustom (the son of) Dorabjee, who, for the assistance he gave the English in 1692 against the Seedee of Junjeera, was created, by *sanad* (*i.e.* patent), *patel* (*i.e.* mayor) of the Coolees of Bombay.

The Parsee Ashburners derive their patronymic from an ancestor in the early part of the late century, the friend and associate of a well-known English gentleman then resident in Western India. The Bhownaggrees take their name from an ancestor, a wealthy *jaghirdar*, who in 1744 built a tank of solid stone for public use at Bhavnagar in Kattyawar, and also from their later official connection with this well-known "model Native State." The Jamsetjee Jejeebhoys and Comasjee Jehanghiers derive their double-barreled surnames from the first baronet and knight, respectively, of these two eminent Parsee families. Other well-known Parsee surnames are Albless, Bahadurjee, Banajee, Bengalee, Bhandoo-pwala, Bharda, Cama (or Kama), Dadysett, Damanwala, Gamadia, Gazdar, Ghandi, Kapadia, Karaka, Khabrajee, Kharagat, Kohiyar, Marzban, Modee, Petit (Sir Dinshaw Manockjee Petit, first baronet of this name), Panday, Parak, Sanjana, Sayar, Seth, Sethna, Shroff, Talyarkan, Wadia. Some of their surnames are very eccentric, such as Doctor, Ready-money, Solicitor, etc., and should be abolished. There is actually a Dr. Solicitor.

˙ The interesting point about the Parsee surnames is that when first introduced, through the influence of their close contact with the English, they were not absolutely hereditary, but were changed after a generation or two. Thus the present Bhownaggrees used, at one time, the surname of Compadore, from the office so designated held by one of their ancestors under the Portuguese.

The Hindoos have always had surnames, and jealously guard their authenticity and continuity in the traditions of their families, although they do not, even yet in Western India, universally use them in public. Their personal and paternal names are derived, among the higher castes, from the names of the gods, the thousand and one names of Vishnoo and Seeva, of Ganesha, etc., and from the names of well-known mythological heroes, historical saints, etc., the name selected being one the initial of which indicates the lunar asterism (*nakshatra*) under which the child (*i.e.* a son) is born ; but their surnames have a tribal, or, as in the case of the Parsees, a local, or official, or some other merely accidental, origin.

If, then, we had only to deal with the Hindoos and Parsees, they might be readily indexed under their surnames. But when we come to the Indian Mussulmans the problem is at once seen to be beset with perplexities which seem to me impossible to unravel. The Indian Mussulmans—indeed all *muslimin*—are classified as Sayeds, Sheikhs, Mo(n)gols, and Pathans. The Sayeds (literally, "nobles," "lords") are the descendants of the Prophet Mahomet, through his

son-in-law Allee; those descended through
Fatima being distinguished as Sayed
Hussanee and Sayed Hooseinee, and
those from his other wives as Sayed Allee.
The first name given to a Mussulman of
this class is the *quasi*-surname Sayed or
Meer (also, literally, "nobleman," " lord "),
followed by the personal name and the
paternal name; but these *quasi*-surnames
often fall into disuse after manhood has
been reached.

The Sheikhs (literally, "chiefs "),—and
all *muslimin* descended from Mahomet and
Aboo Bukeer and Oomur are Sheikhs,—
have one or other of the following surnames placed before or after their personal
and paternal names: Abd, Allee, Bukhs,
Goolam, Khoaja, Sheikh. But as Sayeds
are also all Sheikhs, they sometimes, on
attaining manhood, assume the surname
of Sheikh, dropping that of Sayed, or
Meer, given to them at birth.

The Mo(n)gols, whether of the Persian
(Eranee) sect of Sheeahs, or the Turkish
(Tooranee) sect of Soonnees, have placed
before, or after, their personal and paternal
names, one or other of the following

surnames : Aga ("lord"), Beg ("lord"),
Meerza, and Mo(n)gol. But in Persia
both Sayeds and Sheikhs assume, instead
of their proper patronymics, the surname of
Aga, or Beg, or Mo(n)gol; while Mo(n)gols
whose mothers are Sayeds are given the
pre, or post, surname of Meerza.

The Pathans have the surname Khan
("lord") placed invariably after their
personal and paternal names. But Sayeds
and Sheikhs often have the word Khan
placed after their class, personal, and
paternal names—not, however, as a surname, but as a complimentary or substantial
title, pure and simple.

Again, all classes of *muslimin*, and the
Hindoos also, and even the Parsees, are in
the habit of adding all sorts of complimentary and substantial titles both before
and after their names. How, then, is it
possible to apply any one rightly reasoned
rule to the indexing of such names, or
any but the arbitrary rule of thumb :—to
index them in the order in which the bearer
of them places them in his signature to
letters, cheques, and other documents?
This gets over all the embarrassing

difficulties created by the paraphernalia of a
man's official designations, complimentary
—or substantial, titles, etc.   Take, for
example, this transcript of a hypothetical
Hindoo official's visiting-card :
    " Dewan Sahib " (official and courtesy
titles).
    " Rajashri " (special social title).
    " A." (personal name).
    " B." (paternal name).
    " Z." (family or true surname).
    No Englishman unfamiliar with the
etiquettes of Indian personal nomencla-
ture could possibly index such a card
as this with intelligent correctness.   But
this Hindoo gentleman would simply sign
himself in a private letter, " A. B. Z."
(*i.e.* A., the son of B., of the clan of Z.),
and so he should be indexed.
    The personal names of *muslimin* also
have for the most part an astronomical
association, being generally selected from
those beginning with the initial or finial
letter of the name of the planet ruling
the day on which the child (*i.e.* a son)
is born.
    I presume that what I have here said

of the methods of naming the Indian Mussulmans also applies to the *muslimin* of Persia and Central Asia and Turkey and Arabia ; but beyond these countries I have no information as to the methods of naming people in the other Oriental Indies, such as Ceylon, Burmah, China, and Japan.

As to the transliteration of Oriental personal names, I always accept that followed by the person bearing them.

I have put the matter as briefly as possible, and almost too briefly for absolute accuracy of expression ; and it will be noted I say nothing of local exceptions to the general rule regulating Hindoo names of persons ; and, again, nothing of female names, Hindoo, Mussulmanee, or Parsee.

GEORGE BIRDWOOD.

January 9, 1902.

CHAPTER VII.

How to Set About the Index.

" And thus by God's assistance we have finished
our Table. Miraculous almost was the execution
done by David on the Amalekites who saved
neither man nor woman alive to bring tidings to
Gath. I cannot promise such exactness in our
Index, that no name hath escaped our enquiry :
some few, perchance, hardly slipping by, may
tell tales against us. This I profess, I have not,
in the language of some modern quartermaster,
wilfully burnt towns, and purposely omitted
them ; and hope that such as have escaped our
discovering, will only upon examination appear
either not generally agreed on, by authors, for
proper names, or else by proportion falling
without the bounds of Palestine, Soli Deo
gloria."—Thomas Fuller.

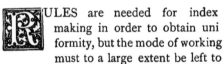ULES are needed for index
making in order to obtain uni
formity, but the mode of working
must to a large extent be left to
the indexer. Most of us have our own

172

favourite ways of doing things, and it is therefore absurd to dictate to others how to set to work. If we employ any one to do a certain work, we are entitled to expect it to be well done ; but we ought to allow the worker to adopt his own mode of work. Some men will insist not only on the work being well done, but also upon their way of doing it. This takes the spirit out of the worker, and is therefore most unwise.

Still, I have found that those who are unaccustomed to index work are anxious to be informed how to proceed. The following notes are therefore only intended as hints for the use of those who wish for them, and need not be acted upon if the reader has a plan that he finds better suited for his purpose. Two essentially different kinds of index must be considered first : (1) There is the index which is always growing ; and (2) there is the index that is made at one time, and is printed immediately it is ready for the press. The same course of procedure will not be suitable for both these classes.

1. Indexes to commonplace books belong to this category. It has been usual here to leave a few pages blank for the index, and to arrange the entries in strict alphabetical order under the first letters and then under the first vowel following a consonant, or the second, when the initial is a vowel. This is highly inconvenient and confusing, especially when words without a second vowel, as *Ash* and *Epps*, are placed at the head of each letter, *Ash* coming before *Adam* and *Abel*, and *Epps* before *Ebenezer*. It is better to spare a few more pages for the index, and plan the alphabet out so that the entries may come in their correct alphabetical order. Unfortunately the blank index is usually set out according to this absurd vowel system. Commonplace books are now, however, very much out of fashion. A better system of note-keeping is to use paper of a uniform size, to write each distinct note on a separate sheet of paper, and to fasten the slips of paper together by means of clips. If this plan is adopted, the notes are much more easily consulted,

and they can be rearranged as often as is necessary. Now the index can be made on cards, or a special alphabeticised * book can be set aside for the purpose. Cards of a uniform size, kept in trays or boxes, are very convenient for the purpose of making an ever-growing index. You can make a general index in one alphabet, and when you have any special subject on hand, you can choose out the particular cards connected with that subject, and arrange them in a distinct alphabet. When the distinct alphabet is no longer required, the cards can be rearranged in the general alphabet. Cards are unquestionably the most convenient for an index that is ever changing in volume and in form. Rearrangement can be made without the trouble of re-writing the entries.

2. For an index which is made straight off at one time, and sent to the printer

* Some may consider this a monstrous word; but it conveys a convenient description of blank books with the alphabet marked on the leaves of the book either cut in or with tablets projecting from the margin.

when finished, foolscap paper is probably the most convenient to use. The pages as written upon can be numbered, and this will relieve the mind of the indexer of fear that any of these should be lost. The numbering will serve till the time comes for the index to be cut up and arranged.

Some indexers use separate slips of a uniform size, or cards, with a single entry on each slip. Although this plan has the advantage that you can keep your index in alphabetical order as you go along, which is sometimes convenient for reference, it is, on the whole, a cumbersome one for an index, although it is almost essential for a catalogue.

In the present day when paper is so cheap, it is well to use fresh sheets all of the same size—either quarto post or foolscap. Some persons are so absurdly economical as to use the blank sides of used paper, such as envelopes, etc., so that their manuscript is of all sizes and will never range. It is necessary to warn such persons that they lose more time by the inconvenient form of their paper than they gain by not buying new material.

In general practice the most convenient plan is to make your index straight on, using the paper you have chosen. Another plan is to use a portfolio of parchment with an alphabet cut on the leaves, and with guards to receive several leaves of foolscap under each letter. Thus every entry can be written at once in first letters. Where there are many large headings this is very convenient, and time is saved by entering the various references on the same folio without the constant repetition of the same heading Possibly the most convenient method is to unite the two plans. Those references which we know to belong to large headings can be entered on the folios in the alphabetical guard-book, and the rest can be written straight through on the separate leaves.

Before commencing his work, the indexer must think out the plan and the kind of index he is to produce ; he will then consider how he is to draw out the references.

Whatever system is adopted, it is well to bear in mind that the indexer should obtain some knowledge of the book he is about to index before he sets to work. The following remarks by Lord Thring may be applied to other subjects than law :

" A complete knowledge of the whole *law* is required before he begins to make the index, for until he can look down on the entire field of law before him, he cannot possibly judge of the proper arrangement of the headings or of the relative importance of the various provisions."

During his work the indexer must constantly ask himself what it is for which the consulter is likely to seek. The author frequently uses periphrases to escape from the repetition of the same fact in the same form, but these periphrases will give little information when inserted as headings in an index; and it is in this point of selecting the best catchword that the good indexer will show his superiority over the commonplace worker.

This paramount characteristic of the good indexer is by no means an easy one to acquire. When the indexer is absorbed in the work upon which he is working, he takes for granted much with which the consulter coming fresh to the subject is not familiar. The want of this characteristic is most marked in the case of the bad indexer.

In printing references to the entries in an index it is important to make a distinction between the volume and the page; this is done best by printing the number of the volumes in Roman letters and the page in Arabic numerals. When, however, the volumes are numerous, the Roman letters become cumbersome, and mistakes are apt to occur, so that one is forced to use Arabic numerals; and in order to distinguish between volume and page, the numbers of the volumes must be printed in solid black type.

When a book is often reprinted in different forms it would be well to refer to chapters and paragraphs, so that the same index would do for all editions. The paragraphs in Dr. Jessopp's edition of North's *Lives of the Norths* are numbered, but they are not numbered throughout. The references are very confusing and

require a key. Thus, P stands for Preface ;
F for Life of the Lord Keeper ; D, Life of
Dudley ; J, Life of Dr. John ; R, Autobio-
graphy of Roger, and also Notes ; R L,
Letters from Lady North ; R I, Letters
from Roger North ; and S, Supplementary.
In the Letters the references are to pages
and not to paragraphs. With such a
complicated system, one is tempted to
leave the index severely alone. This is
the more annoying in that the index is
not a long one, and the pages might have
been inserted without any great trouble.

Much confusion has been caused by
reprinting an index for one edition in a
later one without alteration. An instance
may be given by citing the reprint of
Whitelock's *Memorials,* published at the
University Press, Oxford, in 1853. The
original edition is in one volume folio
(1682, reprinted 1732), and the new
edition is in four volumes octavo. But to
save expense the old index was printed
to the new book. The difficulty was in
part got over by giving the pages of the
1732 edition in the margin ; but as may
be imagined, it is a most troublesome

business to find anything by this means.
Moreover, the old index is not a good
one, but thoroughly bad, with all the
old misprints retained in the new edition.
As a specimen of the extreme inaccuracy
of the compilation, it may be mentioned
that under one heading of thirty-four
entries Mr. Edward Peacock detected
seven blunders. Although Mr. Peacock
had no statistics of the other entries,
his experience led him to believe that
if any heading were taken at random,
about one in four of the entries would
be found to be misprinted.

In the case of a large index it is
necessary to take into consideration the
greatly increased work connected with
arrangement. The amount of this may
be said to increase in geometrical rather
than in arithmetical progression. When
the indexer comes to the last page of a
great book he rejoices to have finished
his work ; but he will find by experience,
when he calculates the arrangement
of his materials, that he has scarcely
done more than half of what is before
him.

If cards or separate slips are used, these will only need to be arranged for the press ; but if sheets of paper have been, written upon, these will have to be cut up. There is little to be said about this, but it is worth giving the hint that much time is saved if shears or large scissors are used, so that the whole width of paper may be severed in two cuts.

In the case of a small index there is little difficulty with material, for it can be arranged at once into first letters, and when the table is cleared of the slips these can be placed in the pages of an ordinary book to keep them distinct, and can then be sorted in perfect alphabet and pasted down. In the case of a large index it will be necessary to place the slips in a safer place. Large envelopes are useful receptacles for first letters ; and when the slips are placed in them, the indexer will feel at ease and sure that none will be lost.

It is well to go through the whole of the envelopes of first letters and sort the slips into second and third letters before the pasting is commenced, so that you may know that the order is correct, or make such alterations as are necessary before it is too late. The final perfect alphabetical arrangement can be made when the slips are placed on the table ready to be pasted.

The sorting of slips into alphabetical order seems a simple matter which scarcely needs any particular directions; still such have been made.

The late Mr. Charles F. Blackburn, who had had a considerable experience, gave some instruction for sorting slips in his *Hints on Catalogue Titles* (1884). He wrote :

" Having never seen in print any directions for putting titles into alphabetical order, I venture to describe the system I have been accustomed to use. First sort the entire heap into six heaps, which will lie before you thus :

A—D	E—H	I—M
N—R	S	T—Z.

Then take the heap A—D and sort it into its component letters, after which each letter can be brought into shape by use of the plan first applied to the whole alphabet. It is best to go on with the

second process until you have the whole
alphabet in separate letters, because if
you brought A, for example, into its component parts and put them into alphabetical order, you might not impossibly find
some A's among the later letters—one of
the inevitable accidents of sorting quickly.
With this hint or two the young cataloguer
will easily find his way ; and various de-
vices for doing this or that more handily
are sure to suggest themselves in the
course of practice. The great thing is
to be started."

The latter part of this extract is good
advice, but I think it is a mistake to make
two operations of the sorting in first letters,
for it can be done quite easily in one.

The following suggestion made by Mr.
Blackburn is a good one, and is likely to
save the very possible mixture of some
of the heaps :

"In my own practice I have got into
a way of letting the slips fall on the
table at an angle of forty-five degrees.
Then, if the accumulation of titles should
cause the heaps to slide, they will run
into one another distinct, so that they

can be separated instantly without sorting afresh."

I have never myself found any difficulty in sorting out into first letters at one time, and it soon becomes easy to place the slips in their proper heaps without any thought. Mr. F. B. Perkins, of the Boston Public Library, however, in his paper on "Book Indexes" gives some good directions which are worth quoting here :

"Next alphabet them by initial letters. This process is usually best done by using a diagram or imaginary frame of five rows of five letters each, on which to put the titles at this first handling. The following arrangement of printers' dashes will show what I mean. (The letters placed at the left hand of the first row and right hand of the last indicate well enough where the rest belong.)

```
A ——  ——  ——  ——  —— U
B ——  ——  ——  ——  —— V
C ——  ——  ——  ——  —— W
D ——  ——  ——  ——  —— X
E ——  ——  ——  ——  —— YZ." *
```

* *Public Libraries in the United States.* Special Report. Part I., 1876, p. 730.

When the alphabetical arrangement is completed so far as the indexer considers it necessary for his purpose, it is time to think of the pasting down of the slips. This can be done in several ways, and the operator will doubtless choose that which suits him best. As already remarked, men will always find out the way most agreeable to themselves, and it is unwise to insist on others following our way in preference to their own.

The human mind is capable of interesting itself in almost anything it may undertake; but indexing cannot be other than hard work, and it is unfair to make it harder by fixing unnecessary limits. The worker is always happier at his work if he is allowed to do it in his own way.

The first thing to settle is as to the paper upon which the index is to be pasted. A very large-sized paper is inconvenient, and foolscap or quarto is the best for constant handling,—all the pages should be of exactly the same size. Sometimes it is necessary to have a small margin, but generally the width of the paper used for the index should be followed. There is no greater mistake than to study economy in the use of paper for pasting on. Some persons have facilities for the use of wastepaper that has been printed on on one side, and, not having been used, is in good order and of equal size. Some persons cut up newspapers, but this is a practice not to be recommended, not only on account of the print, but because the paper is generally so abominably bad and tearable. If the wastepaper referred to above is not within reach, it is well to buy a good printing-paper, which can be cut into the size required. There are, however, many cheap papers already machine-cut into the size required, which can easily be obtained.

Some with the love of saving strong upon them cut up newspapers into lengths of about four inches wide, and paste the slips upon these, with the result that all the ragged ends give continual trouble, and are apt to be torn away. Of all savings, this is the most ill-advised.

Although the "copy" is to be printed from at once, and will soon become useless, it is a great comfort to have material that is convenient to handle while it is required. Some thought may also be given to the compositor, whose life will be made a burden to him if you send him "copy" with all the ends loose. It is also well to keep the pages as flat as possible, so that a heap of these do not wobble about, but keep together smooth and tidy.

Sometimes it may be desirable to paste only on half the paper, so as to have room for additional entries. If this is done, the side must be altered periodically, or the pages with slip about and give endless trouble.

When the index is in course of arrangement the greatest care must be taken that none of the slips are lost, for such a loss is almost irreparable—first because you do not know when a slip goes astray; and even if you do know of your loss it is almost impossible to remedy it, as you have no clue to the place from which the slip came.

There will always be anxiety to the indexer while his work is being cut up and sorted. A breeze from a window when a door is opened may blow some of his slips away. Too many of the slips should not be allowed on the table at one time, and the indexer will feel the greatest comfort when he knows that his slips are safely reposing in their several envelopes. All queries should also be kept in envelopes, and each envelope should be inscribed with a proper description of its contents. When the slips are pasted down they are safe—that is if they have been affixed securely to the paper.

Having made these general observations, we may now proceed to consider how to paste. It seems a very simple matter, that requires no directions ; but even here a few remarks may not be out of place.

When your paper is ready in a pile of about fifty pages, each page numbered in its proper sequence, you can proceed to work. For the purpose of laying down slips on uniform pages at one time, paste is the only satisfactory material. Gum will only be used by the inexperienced. It cannot be used satisfactorily on large surfaces, like paste, and when it oozes up between the slips it is stickier and does more damage in fixing the pages together than paste does. You might as well fix paperhangings on your walls with gum.

As to paste, if you have a long job on hand it is better to have it made at home, of a good consistency, but not too thick. It ought to run freely from the brush. A good cook will make good paste, but if you are specially particular you can make it yourself. If you require it to last for any time, you must add a little alum ; but when you have a big index before you, you will use a bowl of paste in an evening, and there is therefore no question as to keeping.

" Stickphast " is a very good material ; it sticks well and keeps well, and it is an excellent adjunct to the writing-table, but it is not suitable for pasting down a long index. It is too dear, it is too thick, and it is too lumpy. If the paste

is made at home, it need not be lumpy ;
and lumps, when you are pasting, are
irritating to the last degree.

The paper and the paste being ready,
with a fair-sized brush to spread the
paste, we come to consider how best to
proceed with the work in hand. You
require a good-sized table,—a large board
on tressels in an empty room is the best,
but a dining-table will serve. At the
extreme right of the table you place the
batch of paper upon which you are about
to paste, and then sort your slips in
perfect order, ranging them in columns
from right to left. The object of thus
going backwards is to save you from
passing over several columns as you take
the slips off the table, and, instead, going
straight on. You can push your batch
of paper on as the various columns suc-
cessively disappear. More slips should
not be set out than you can paste at
one sitting, as it is not well to leave the
slips loose on the table. Of course, you
can paste from the left side if you wish,
and then the columns will range from
left to right ; but this is not so convenient

for continued arrangement of the columns of slips as you require them.

There are more ways than one in placing the paste upon the paper; the most usual way is to paste down the two sides of the paper just the width of the slips, and some add a stroke down the middle. Another way is to put a plentiful supply of paste on a page or board, and then to place the back of each slip upon this. If you place your fingers on the two ends and press them towards the middle, the slip will be ready to be placed in its proper position, having taken up just sufficient paste. A still different plan is to paste the board or paper as in the previous case, and then place the face of the whole page on this. You then take it off, and, placing the dry side on the batch of paper, proceed to affix the slips to it. The advantage of the two last processes is that the paper is not so wet as in the first-mentioned plan, and in consequence the paper does not curl so much, but lies flatter. In the first place the sheets must be set out separately on the floor to dry, so that they may not stick together, but this is not so necessary in the two latter processes.

Some indexers strongly object to pasting. This was the case with Mr. E. H. Malcolm, who wrote thus to *Notes and Queries* :

" I long ago discovered the cause of imperfections in my own work. It was the ' cutting into slips ' and ' laying down ' processes. The fact is you cannot be sure of preserving the cuttings or slips, if very numerous ; they are almost certain to get mixed or lost, or elude you somehow. My remedy is this. I now take cheap notepaper and write one entry only on each leaf. Having compiled my index thus from A to Z, I arrange my slips and manipulate them as I would a pack of cards, although shuffling only for the purpose of getting the arrangement of the letters right. Thus I save myself all the labour and trouble of pasting or laying down the slips in analytical order. I do not mind a little extra expenditure of paper by only entering one item on every slip, for I am compensated for the appearance of bulk by finding that I have secured order and arrangement free from the consequences of a finical arrangement of the slips and a dirty and tiresome labour of pasting down." *

As already pointed out in these pages, Mr. Malcolm is quite right respecting slips for a growing index ; but when it comes to sending the "copy" to the printer the case is different.   Here there is more safety in the pasted down slips, which are less likely to be lost than the loose ones even when numbered.

As you proceed in your work you may wish to know how far your index agrees with other indexes in its proportion of letters, and to calculate what proportion of the whole you have already done.

Some calculations as to the relative extent of the different letters have been made.   Thus B is the largest letter in an index of proper names, but loses its pre-eminence in an index of subjects ; and S takes high rank in both classes.

Mr. F. A. Curtis,† of the Eagle

* 5th S., vi. 114 (1876).
† *Assurance Magazine*, vol. viii., 1860, pp. 54-7.

Insurance Office, made in 1858 a calculation of the relative proportions of the
different letters of the alphabet in respect
to proper names. He described his object
in a letter entitled, "On the Best Method
of Constructing an Index." He wrote
that, having had occasion to construct an
index of the lives assured in the " Eagle "
Company, he had drawn up a few
observations upon the subject. " The
requirements of an index and the proportions of its several parts are the two
principal questions to be considered.
Under the first head it may be observed
that the index of a company upon a large
scale should afford as much abstract
information as possible. Those who
refer to it do so with different views,
for the objects of their inquiry must
necessarily vary with their respective
duties. It is therefore desirable that the
index should be constructed with a view
to provide for the wants of each person,
so far, at least, as to enable him to obtain
information in the most direct way; and
it will be proper to insert in the index
particulars some of which do not usually

find a place in such a book. Let it be supposed that an individual signing his name ' J. Smith' inquires about the bonus, premium, or assignment, etc., of his policy, without stating either number, date, or amount. This is not an unusual case, and it will serve to illustrate my meaning by showing the nature of the difficulties which have to be encountered. J. may stand for John, James, Joseph, etc. There will probably be many of each kind in connection with the like surname, and it would be very difficult to discover, without a tedious investigation, to which policy J. Smith refers, unless the individuality of each person recorded in the index under that name be distinctly shown. The 'locality' of the assurance might be adopted as a mark of distinction ; and we should in many instances be able to fix upon the right name by simply comparing the address of the writer with the place where the policy was effected."

This is a most valuable suggestion to all indexers. Many persons, to save trouble at the time, write initials instead of full Christian names. It should be a rule always to write these in full. When the index comes to be printed, the Christian names can be contracted if it is necessary to save space. The most important matter in the arrangement of an index is to avoid the confusion of two persons as one, and the possibility of making this blunder is greatly increased by the use of initials instead of full names. In the *British Museum Catalogue* it has been found necessary in many cases to add particulars to distinguish between men with the same names.

Mr. Curtis goes on to say :

" With regard to the second part of this subject—*i.e.* the proportions of the several parts of the index—I may observe that the most useful mode of division appears to me to be that which is adopted by many offices—namely, to classify the surname under its first letter, and to subdivide according to the first vowel thereafter, adopting the first subdivision for such names as 'Ash,' 'Epps,' etc., which have no succeeding vowel."

This, however, is a very unnatural arrangement, and has been, I believe, very generally given up. It is therefore unnecessary to refer further to Mr. Curtis's calculations of the proportions of the vowels in the subdivisions. Calculations can be made for the subdivision of the complete alphabet with a better result. Of course, in the case of initial vowels the following consonants have most to be considered, and in initial consonants the following vowels. Mr. Curtis's calculations respecting the first letters of surnames are of much value. He used the commercial lists of the *Post Office London Directory*, and compared them with Liverpool, Hull, Manchester, Sheffield, Birmingham, and Bristol directories, and with three lists of different assurance companies ; and after making his calculations from nearly 233,000 surnames, he found the total average very similar in its result. Mr. William Davis made similar calculations from the *Clergy List*, which came out much the same. These he contributed to *Notes and Queries*,* and subsequently he made a further calculation from French names.†

* 2nd S., vi. 496.   † 3rd S., iv. 371.

I have united these results in one table
as follows :

		MR. CURTIS.	CLERGY LIST.	FRENCH NAMES.
A	...	3·1	3·1	2·9
B	...	10·9	11·3	11·5
C	...	8·5	7·9	9·2
D	...	4·3	4·7	10·7
E	...	2·4	2·5	0·9
F	...	3·6	3·1	3·9
G	...	5·1	4·6	7·4
H	...	8·6	9·3	3·5
I, J	...	3·2	3·5	2·4
K	...	2·0	1·8	6·4
L	...	4·7	4·3	10·8
M	...	6·7	6·9	8·8
N	...	2·0	1·6	1·2
O	...	1·0	1·1	0·6
P	...	5·9	6·1	6·7
Q	...	0·2	0·0	0·3
R	...	4·6	4·4	5·3
S	...	9·7	7·7	4·3
T	...	4·0	4·4	3·3
U, V	...	1·0	1·3	3·2
W	...	7·9	8·3	0·8
X	...	0·0	0·0	0·0
Y	...	0·5	0·4	0·1
Z	...	0·1	0·0	0·0

It will be noticed that B is strongest
in all three, and C is fairly equal. S is
smaller in French names, but probably
would be much larger in German names.
H and W are also much smaller in
French, while D and L are much
larger. The preponderance of the latter
letters is of course caused by the large
number of names beginning with *De*
and *La*.

Indexes are not confined to proper
names, and therefore it is necessary to
add some calculations as to the proportions
of the several letters in indexes of subjects.
The following table is formed from three
large indexes, each different in character.
I. represents Gough's *Index to the Publications of the Parker Society*, which
may be taken as a very good standard
index. The subjects are very varied, and
there are no specially long headings ; it
also contains proper names as well as
subjects. II. represents an index of
subjects in Civil Engineering which contains a good number of large headings.
III. represents the index to the Minutes
of a public board, and also contains a

considerable proportion of large headings. It will be seen that the numbers vary so considerably as to be of very little practical value. The percentages are, I think, interesting, but they show conclusively that indexes will vary so considerably that in order to obtain a satisfactory percentage a separate calculation will have to be made in each case. Large headings will vitiate any average; in fact, I have lately had to do with an index in which R was the largest letter, on account of such extensive headings as *Railways* and *Roads*.

One striking point in the averages is that B is found to be displaced from the pre-eminent position it occupies in the percentages of proper names.

		I.	II.	III.
A	...	10·67	2·63	5·58
B	...	6·94	5·07	6·28
C	...	15·63	8·26	8·84
D	...	2·48	4·50	4·65
E	...	3·23	6·94	11·39
F	...	2·85	3·38	1·63
G	...	4·34	3·56	1·86

	I.	II.	III.
H ...	4·34	3·19	2·09
I ...	1·74	2·72	1·39
J ...	3·97	0·14	0·46
K ...	0·74	0·05	0·23
L ...	5·58	4·97	15·12
M ...	5·71	5·82	7·67
N ...	1·37	0·19	0·93
O ...	1·74	1·31	1·63
P ...	9·31	6·75	7·67
Q ...	0·12	0·94	0·47
R ...	2·48	12·38	8·14
S ...	8·44	13·32	8·14
T ...	3·60	5·72	1·40
U ...	0·50	0·05	0·47
V ...	0·99	0·61	2·33
W ...	2·61	7·41	1·51
X ...	0·03	0·00	0·00
Y ...	0·22	0·00	0·00
Z ...	0·37	0·09	0·06
	100·00	100·00	100·00

When the whole index is pasted down it is not yet ready for the printer, as it will require to be marked for the instruction of the compositor. The printer will have general instructions as to the kind of type to be used and the plan to be adopted, but it will be necessary to mark out those words that are not to be repeated and to insert lines indicating repetition. There are also sure to be little alterations in wording, necessitated by the coming together of the slips, which could not be foreseen when the slips were first written out.

In a large work it is probable that your employers are importunate for " copy," and you will be urged to send this to the printer as you have it ready. If possible, it should be kept to the end, so that you may look over it as a whole, and so see that the same subjects are not in more places than one. You will probably have to make modifications in your plan as you go along, and this may cause difficulties which you will now be able to set right.

Much of the value of an index depends upon the mode in which it is printed, and every endeavour should be made to set it out with clearness. It was not the practice in old indexes to bring the indexed word to the front, but to leave it in its place in the sentence, so that the alphabetical order was not made perceptible to the eye.

There is a great deal to arrange in preparing for the press. Lines of repetition are often a source of blundering, specimens of which have already been given.

The dash should not be too long, and very often space is saved and greater clearness is obtained by putting the general heading on a line by itself, and slightly indenting the following entries.

Black type for headings and for the references to volume and page add much to the clearness of an index, but some persons have a decided objection to the spottiness that is thus given to the page.

Tastes differ so much in respect to printing that it is not possible to indicate the best style to be adopted, and so each must choose for himself. One point, however, is of the greatest importance, and that is where a heading is continued over leaf it should be repeated with the addition of *continued* at the end of the heading. It is not unusual in such cases to see the dash used at the top of the page, which is absurd.

When the index has been put into print, the indexer has still to correct the press, and this is not always an easy matter, as the printer is scarcely likely to have understood all the necessarily elaborate and complicated marks used in preparing for the press. It will therefore still be some time before the end is in sight, and probably the indexer will see cause to agree with my statement on a former page, that in the case of a large index, when the indexing of the book itself is completed, little more than half of the total work is done.

CHAPTER VIII.

General or Universal Index.

" When Baillet, the learned author of the *Jugemens des Savans*, was appointed by M. de Lamoignon keeper of the exquisite library collected by that nobleman, he set to work to compile an index of the contents of all the books contained in it, and this he is said to have completed in August, 1682. After this date, however, the Index continued to grow, and it extended to thirty-two folio volumes, all written by Baillet's own hand."

S knowledge increases and books and magazines gather in number, the need for many indexes becomes daily more evident. We often are certain that something has been written on a subject in which we are interested, but in vain we seek for a clue to it. We want a key to all this ever-increasing literature.

As long ago as 1842 the late Thomas Watts, of the British Museum, one of the most learned and all-knowing of librarians, spoke to the late Dr. Greenhill of Hastings on the need for the formation of an Index Society. This date I give on the authority of Dr. Greenhill. Mr. Watts was a perfect index in himself, and few inquirers sought information from him which his fully stored mind was not able to supply; and he was not jealous of the printed index, as some authorities are. Twelve years after —in 1854—an announcement was made in *Notes and Queries* of the projected formation of a "Society for the Formation of a General Literary Index." In the 2nd Series, vol. i., p. 486, the late Mr. Thomas Jones, who signed himself "Bibliothecar. Chetham.," commenced a series of articles, which he continued for several years, as a contribution to this general index; but nothing more was heard of the society. Inquiries were made in various numbers of *Notes and Queries*, but no response was obtained. In 1876 a contributor to the same

periodical, signing himself "A. H.," proposed the formation of a staff of index
compilers. In 1874 the late Professor
Stanley Jevons published his *Principles of
Science.* In the chapter on Classification
he enlarged on the value of indexes, and
added :

"The time will perhaps come when
our views upon this subject will be extended, and either Government or some
public society will undertake the systematic
cataloguing and indexing of masses of
historical and scientific information,
which are now almost closed against
inquiry" (1st ed., vol. ii., p. 405 ; 2nd
ed., p. 718).

In the following year Mr. Edward Solly
and I, without having then seen this
passage, consulted as to the possibility of
starting an Index Society, but postponed
the actual carrying out of the scheme for
a time.   In July of this same year, 1875,
Mr. J. Ashton Cross argued in a pamphlet
that a universal index might be formed
by co-operation through a clearing-house,
and would pay if published in separate
parts.   In September, 1877, some letters

by Mr. W. J. Thoms, who signed himself "A Lover of Indexes," were published in the *Pall Mall Gazette*, in which the foundation of an Index Society was strongly urged. In October, 1877, Mr. Cross read a paper before the Conference of Librarians, which was a revival of the scheme previously suggested. Mr. Robert Harrison, late Secretary of the London Library, in a report of the Conference of Librarians published in the *Athenæum* for October 13th, 1877, wrote :

Could not a permanent Index Society be founded with the support of voluntary contributions of money as well as of subject matter ? In this way a regular staff could be set to work, under competent direction, and could be kept steadily at work until its performances became so generally known and so useful as to enable it to stand alone and be self-supporting. Many readers would readily jot down the name of any new subject they met with in the book before them, and the page on which it occurs, and forward their notes to be sorted and

14

arranged by any society that would undertake the work."

Mr. Justin Winsor, the late distinguished librarian of Harvard University, writing to the *Athenæum*, said :

"We have been in America striving for years to get some organised body to undertake this very work."

Following on all this correspondence, the Index Society was founded ; but after doing some useful work it was amalgamated with the Index Library founded by Mr. Phillimore, having failed from want of popular support. This want of permanent success was probably owing to its aim being too general. Those who were interested in one class of index cared little for indexes which were quite different in subject.

I fear that the interest of the public in the production of indexes (which is considerable) does not go to the length of willingness to pay for these indexes, which from the fewness of those who care for these helps must always be expensive. When suggestions were made in *Notes and Queries* for the compilation and publication of certain needed indexes, Mr. J. Cuthbert Welch wrote that the editor of a journal offered to publish an index if he could obtain sufficient subscribers. Respecting this offer, the publisher said, "Altogether I had six offers to take one copy each." This rebuff caused Mr. Welch to say, "Is it not rather that people are not energetic to buy such indexes than that publishers are not energetic enough to issue them?" *

There is still a great want for indexes of history and biography, and it is probable that if the objects of the Index Society had been confined to these it might have been more successful. In November, 1878, Mr. Edward Solly wrote a letter to me in which he sketched out a very important scheme for a biographical index which would be of the greatest value. He wrote:

"I do not think the Index Society can take up any subject of greater utility, or one more likely to be of service to the general public as well as students, than

* 8th S., i. 364.

an Index of Biographies. An entire
index of all known lives would obviously
be much too large an undertaking ; we can
only attempt a part of the subject. Probably in the first instance we should do
well to try and form an index of British
lives ; such a work would I think, if
tolerably complete, certainly fill at least
ten large octavo volumes.

"The work might be considerably
diminished in bulk if we were to deter-
mine to leave out all names now to be
found in certain standard works such as
Chalmers' Biographical Dictionary. It
is evident, however, that to do this would
greatly diminish the value of our index,
and would cause us to put aside hundreds
of memoranda which it is most important
to index, I mean references to more recent
notes, memoirs, letters and anecdotes,
which are to be met with in journals and
lives, and which often throw new and
important light on older published
Biographies.

"It is on account of these difficulties
that I would propose that we endeavour
to undertake an index of Biographical

references of persons who have died in a certain given period—say 1800-1825, or 1800-1850, or perhaps 1750-1800.

" With a view to this I should like to see lists made of all Biographical matters in such books as the Gentleman's Magazine, European Magazine, Monthly Magazine, Anti-Jacobin Magazine, etc Also such books as the Annual Necrology, Public Characters, Living Authors, etc., and thirdly of references to Biographical Memoranda dispersed throughout Lives and Memoirs such as ' Kilvert's Memoirs,' I mean books in which no one from the title would expect to find such information."

It will be seen that such an index as is here sketched would be an inestimable help to the student. It would form a useful supplement to the *Dictionary of National Biography*, for it must be remembered that such an index would contain a majority of references to men and women whose claims to distinction or notoriety do not attain to the standard set up by the promoters of that grand work. Possibly, if such an index was undertaken by co-operation as an object in itself, and not as one among other subjects, it might be compiled in one alphabet instead of in periods, which would make it much more valuable for reference. Naturally the great advantage of periods is that, if left incomplete, what is published (if it covers a period) will always be of value, while a portion of the alphabet would be almost worthless.

The Rev. John E. B. Mayor has collected a great mass of biographical references which are of much value. In an interesting communication on his indexes he suggests the formation of a British Biographical Society which might be called the Antony Wood Society.*

There is one project of the Index Society which has never been undertaken, but which is still wanted as much as ever—*viz.* a general or universal index. Some think this to be an impossibility, and that to attempt its preparation is a waste of time. Those who hold this opinion have not sufficient faith in the simplicity and usefulness of the alphabet.

* *Notes and Queries*, 5th S., xii. 511.

Every one has notes and references of some kind, which are useless if kept unarranged, but, if sorted into alphabetical order, become valuable.

The object of the general index is just this, that anything, however disconnected, can be placed there, and much that would otherwise be lost will there find a resting-place. Always growing and never pretending to be complete, the index will be useful to all, and its consulters will be sure to find something worth their trouble, if not all they may require.

Some attempts have been made at compiling a general index, for what are *Poole's Index, Index of Essays,* Q.P. Indexes, Hetherington's *Index to the Periodicals of the World,* and *Indexes to " The Times,"* but contributions towards a universal index? Such a work as is here proposed can scarcely be carried out unless Government aid is extended to it ; but surely the small amount of money that need be expended upon a sort of general inquiry office would be well laid out !

A sort of skeleton index of universal

information might be drawn up, and this could be added to gradually, partly by specialised effort and partly by the reception of any stray references of interest sent by those who recognise that their notes would find a home. This could be kept in a clearing-house and reference-room.

When the index had become of some importance, and was recognised as a help to the inquirer, it could be printed. When published, it might be interleaved, so that additions might be made which could be sent to the office. Gradually the index would grow into a work of very considerable importance

One of the chief objections to index catalogues of public libraries is that the same work is practically repeated by each library, while a general index would be useful to all. Surely some arrangement might be made by which the various libraries would contribute funds to the central office and receive the indexes, which would serve their purpose as well as those of all the other libraries !

Having said so much, it seems necessary

to explain rather more fully what the general index should contain and what should be omitted. To explain it in a few words, it should be a sort of encyclopædia of references rather than of direct information; but it should contain more headings than any existing encyclopædia. Every one must have felt the want of some book which would give information or references on a large number of subjects that are constantly topics of ordinary conversation, but are consistently ignored in the ordinary books of reference. On the other hand, mere technical references should be omitted, because these details would overload the work, and because specialists have their own sources of information. It is the general information which every one is supposed to possess that is so difficult to obtain.

In the first instance the groundwork of the index should be laid down with care by an expert. All special bibliographies should be entered under their subjects, both those published separately and those included in other books.

Various societies have published indexes.
There are those among the publications
of the Index Society and many others.
The Bibliographical Society has published
indexes to the German periodical
Serapeum and to Dibdin's edition of
Ames' and Herbert's *Typographical
Antiquities* ; but very few persons know
of these books.

The authorities of the British Museum
have given students an immense help
by gathering separate indexes and bibliographies on various subjects into the
dwarf bookcases in the Reading-room.
Here are a large number of aids to knowledge of which the general reader would
have known nothing if they had not so
obligingly been brought under his notice.*

A large number of books contain
special information of importance on
various subjects, the existence of which

* The late Professor Justin Winsor gave a list of
indexes in his useful *Handbook for Readers* (for
the Boston Public Library) ; and I added a
"Preliminary List of Indexes" to *What is an
Index?* London, 1879. Other lists have also
been published by the British Museum, etc.

would never be guessed from the titles.
Attempts at general indexes of special
subjects have been published, such as
F. S. Thomas's *Historical Notes* (1509–
1714), and the main points of these should
be included in the proposed General Index.

When a good groundwork has been
made, the index could be printed; and
doubtless, if this printed index was widely
circulated, a large number of helpers
would speedily be found. Many persons
know of places where full information
on some subject may be found, and
would be glad to place their collections
where they would be helpful to others.

There can surely be no doubt that a
general inquiry office with such an ever-
growing index and a library of printed
indexes would be a boon not only to the
student, but to the general public. Every
day the great truth that keys to knowledge are more and more required is
generally appreciated.

As a groundwork for such a general
index, selection could be made from
the books already mentioned ; and from
the index volumes of Watt's *Bibliotheca*

Britannica (1824), which, with all its faults, is one of the most valuable helps to bibliography, and the subject index of James Darling's *Cyclopædia Bibliographica* (1854–1859), many useful references could be obtained. These two books are gradually getting out of date, but information may be obtained from their pages which is not easily to be obtained elsewhere.

In closing this subject, I feel that too great honour cannot be done to the memory of W. F. Poole, who placed the world under great obligations by the production of his *Index of Periodical Literture*. As far back as 1848, when a student at Yale College, he published an *Index to Subjects treated in the Reviews and other Periodicals* (New York). In 1853 an improved edition was published as the *Index to Periodical Literature*. When Mr. Poole attended the Library Conference at London in 1877 he expressed publicly his pleasure in seeing on the shelves of the British Museum Library a copy of his first index, which he had not seen for some years elsewhere.

He realised that the work, if it were to
be continued, was too great an undertaking for one man, and he succeeded
in arranging for a co-operative index,
which is continued now in several supple-
ments under the able superintendence
of Mr. William I. Fletcher.

An *Index to the " Times"* was started
by J. Giddings in 1862–63, but not continued. Later, Mr. S. Palmer commenced
a *Quarterly Index*, which has been continued forward to the present time, and
also backward. In 1899 Bailey's *Annual
Index to the " Times"* came into being.

The indexing of a paper such as the
Times is a very arduous and difficult
undertaking. In consequence, these indexes cannot be considered as models of
what such works should be.

Mr. Corrie Leonard Thompson criti-
cises in *Notes and Queries* (7th S., x. 345)
the arrangement of the headings of
Palmer's *Index to the " Times"* severely,
but not unfairly. He writes :

" The following are instances of the
absurdities which appear in the volume
just issued (Oct.—Dec. 1842), and will

serve to illustrate the system which has been adopted throughout the index :

"In November, 1842, a floating chapel on the Severn was loosed from its moorings ; this occurrence appears in the index under the heading, ' Disgraceful Act.' Again, referring to the dry weather that was prevailing at the time, the entry is, ' Present Dry Season.' Other references to the same subject are, however, to be found under the heading ' Weather,' which of course is correct.

" A more marked example of carelessness or ignorance of the art of indexing, or both, is that of two women who were committed to Ruthin prison—one, Amelia Home for firing a pistol at a man named Roberts; the other, Jane Williams, for stealing a mare belonging to Robert Owen.   This occurrence is entered under the letter R—' Rather uncommon for Females.'   The chance of any one looking under Rather for an occurrence of this kind must be infinitesimal, to say the least of it ; and so on.   A storm at Saone-et-Loire is indexed under ' Fatal Storm,' and an account of the trial of a small boy for stealing a twopenny pie will be found under 'Atrocious Criminal.' A certain Jane Thomas was so overjoyed at seeing her mother waiting at the stage-door of a theatre that she died in her arms. The employment of capitals is most remarkable, as is also the arrangement of the words, 'Death of Jane Thomas in her Mother's Arms in Holborn at Joy in Seeing her parent at the Stage Door to Receive her.'

"The errors pointed out in these examples, omitting the last instance, as well as the additional fault of indexing under adjectives which have no distinctive feature in them to guide the searcher, evidently arise from the fact that the simple heading of the newspaper article has been taken, without any attempt being made to discover the actual contents of such article."

As already stated on a previous page, it is most important to index the articles in periodicals afresh, and not always to follow the heading of the original. This is of course more particularly the case in respect to newspapers, where the headings are drawn up to catch the reader's eye. The same rule may be insisted on in respect to all indexing, and this is so important that the restatement of it may well conclude this little volume.

In making a general index of several volumes, always index the volumes afresh, and do not be contented with using what has been done before. It is always wiser to put 'new wine into new bottles.'

INDEX.

Bruce's (John) edition of *Historie of Edward IV.*, absurd filling up of initials J. C., 78.

Brunet (G.) translates *White Knight* as *Le Chevalier Blanc*, 77.

Buckland (Dr.) said to be the author of a work *Sur les Ponts et Chaussées*, 77.

Burton (Hill), *Book-Hunter*, allusion to the power in the hands of an indexer, 24.

—— his reference to Prynne's *Histrio-Mastix*, 20.

—— his index to Bentham's *Works*, 102.

CALENDAR as a synonym of index, 7.

Camden Society's publications, Proposed index to, 112.

Campbell (Lady Charlotte) maligned in an index, 81.

Campbell (Lord) proposed punishment for the publication of an indexless book, 82.

—— his confession, 83.

Campkin (Henry), plea for index-makers, 92.

Canadian Journal, bad index, 56.

Capgrave's *Chronicle of England*, blunder in the index, 66.

Cards or separate slips used for indexes, 182.

Carlyle (Thomas), he denounces the putters-forth of indexless books, 82, 91.

—— his reference to Prynne's *Histrio-Mastix*, 15.

—— his remarks on the want of indexes to the standard historical collections, 91.

Catalogue as a synonym of index, 7.

Catalogues, Indexes to, 123.

——of libraries, Indexes to, 123.

Chitty (E.), his supposed grudge against Justice Best, 157.

Christian Observer, Index to, by Macaulay, 91.

Cicero, his use of the word "index," 6, 8.

Clark's (Perceval) index to Trevelyan's *Life of Macaulay*, 95.

Clarke (Mrs. Cowden), her *Concordance to Shakespeare*, 120.

Clarke (William) quoted, 118.

Classification within the alphabet, Evils of, 58, 67.

Cobbett's *Woodlands* quoted, 72.

Coke (Lord Chief Justice) an inaccurate man, 101.

Commonplace books, Indexes to, 174.

Concordances to the Bible, 119.

Concordances to Shakespeare, 120.

Contractions, dangers in filling them out, 78.

Corpus Christi Guild, York, Incomplete index to *The Register of,* 122.

Crestadoro's *Index to the Manchester Free Library Catalogue,* 125.

Cross (J. Ashton), proposal for a universal index, 208, 209.

Cross references not usually popular, 158.

—— curiosities of, 72.

—— want of, in indexes, 70.

Cunningham (Mr.) paid £500 for indexing, 97.

Curll's authors, instructions how to find them, 53.

Curtis (F. A.) on the best method of constructing an index, 195.

Cutter's rule as to the arrangement of peers under their surnames, 146.

Cutting up of entries when written on pages of paper, 182.

" DA," surnames not to be arranged under this prefix, 141.

"Dal" surnames to be arranged under this prefix, 141.

Darling's (James) *Cyclopædia Bibliographica,* Index, 220

Dashes in printing representing repetition to be of uniform length, 161, 204; instances of incorrect use of them, 80, 138.

" De," French surnames not to be arranged under this prefix, 141; English surnames to be arranged under this prefix, 142.

De Quincey on Bentley, 39.

"Del," "Della," surnames to be arranged under these prefixes, 141.

" Des," surnames to be arranged under this prefix, 141.

Dictionary catalogue, its history, 129.

—— Mr. Fortescue's objections to it, 130.

Dictionary makers really indexers, 120.

Disraeli's (Isaac) *Literary Miscellanies* quoted, 1.

Drayton (M.), his use of the word " index," 11.

" Du," surnames to be arranged under this prefix, 141.

Dugdale's *Warwickshire,* the words " index " and " table " both used, 9.

Dumas (Alexandre) *pere et fils,* confused with Alexandre *pere et fils,* harmonium-makers, 24.

Hawkins's *Pleas of the Crown*, Odd cross references in, 75.

Headings, alphabetical arrangement of, 137.

—— instances of bad, 54.

—— printing of, 160.

Henrietta Maria offended with Prynne's *Histrio-Mastix*, 18.

Heskeths, their change of name, 151.

Hetherington's (Miss) opinions on the indexing of periodicals, 59; specimens of absurd references quoted by her, 60; on the qualifications of an indexer, 114.

Hill's (Dr. Birkbeck) admirable indexes, 105-108.

Historical collections, need of indexes to these standard works, 91.

Homer, poetical index to Pope's translation of the Iliad, 21.

House of Commons' Journals, sums paid for the indexes, 97.

Hume (David), index to his *Essays*, 23; he was glad to be saved from the drudgery of making one, 23.

Hunt (Leigh), his opinion on index-making, 26.

—— supposed author of the joke on Best's great mind, 157.

Hutchins's *Dorset*, Separate indexes to, 69.

Hyphen, Use of, in compound names, 149.

I AND J to be kept distinct, 66, 135.

Im Thurn, place of this name in the alphabet, 143.

Index, alphabetical order not at first considered essential, 6; classification to be abjured in an alphabetical index, 58, 67; evils of dividing an index into several alphabets, 69; *General or Universal Index* (chap. viii.), 206, 223; history of the word, 7; use by the Romans, 6; naturalisation of the word in English, 8; introduced into English in the nominative case, 10; *How to Set About the Index* (chap. vii.), 172-205; long struggle with the word "table," 7; soul of a book, *Title-page*; one index to each book, 134; two chief causes of the badness of indexes, 64; varied kinds of, 5.

Index-learning ridiculed, 2.

Index Society, its formation, 210; published index to Trevelyan's *Life of Macaulay*, 95; amalgamation with the Index Library, 210.

King (Dr. William), his
parody of Lister's *Journey
to Paris*, 42.
—— his attack upon Sir
Hans Sloane and the
*Philosophical Transac-
tions*," 42.
—— satirical index to
Bromley's *Travels*, 44
Knowledge, what is true, 1.
"LA," surnames to be
arranged under this pre-
fix, 141.
Lamoignon (M. de), his
library, indexed by
Baillet, 206.
Lawyers good indexers, 98.
"Le," surnames to be ar-
ranged under this prefix,
141.
Library Association, Index
to *Reports*, 113.
Lister's *Journey to Paris*
parodied by Dr. King, 42.
Littré, his derivation of
indice, 10.
London (George), his name
often spelt Loudon, 67.
Longman's Magazine, bad
index, 63.
Loudon (C. J.), the Duke
of Wellington mistakes
his signature for that of
the Bishop of London, 67.
Lowell's *Biglow Papers*,
humorous index, 33.
"M'" AND "Mc" to be
arranged as if written
"Mac," 145.

Macaulay (Lord) an in-
dexer, 91.
—— indexers treated with
contempt by him, 92.
—— his opinion on the
index to his *History*,
93.
—— objection to the indexing of his *History* by a
Tory, 93.
—— his Englishing of
foreign names approved
by Freeman, 144.
—— on Bentley's foibles, 38.
Maine (Duc de), Duc of
Maine, Duke de Maine,
or Duke of Maine, 144.
Malcolm (E. H.) quoted,
193.
Markland (J. H.), remarks
on indexing, 82.
Mayor's (Rev. John E. B.)
collection of biographical
references, 214.
Michel's (Dan) *Ayenbite of
Inwyt*, table of contents, 6.
Minsheu, his use of the
word "index," 9.
Montaigne's *Essays*, index
to Florio's translation,
12.
Moore (Edward) paid
£6400 for indexing, 97.
More (Hannah), Macau-
lay's letter to her, 91.
Morley (John) protests
against indexless books,
84.
Morris (William) on an
absurd cross reference, 72.

Poole's (W. F.) *Index to
Periodical Literature*
quoted, 59; its great value,
220; new edition by co-
operation, 221; his re-
marks on cross references,
71.
Printing of headings, 160;
special type, 160.
P r y n n e, *Histrio-Mastix*,
specimens from the index,
14.
—— a martyr to his con-
scientiousness in making
an index, 15.
Puritans, Prynne's praise
of, 17.
"Pye" as a synonym of
index, 7 (note).
"Pye-book," derivation, 7
(note).

RANKE'S *History of En-
gland*, issue of revised
index by the Clarendon
Press, 113.
Rawlinson (Dr.) on the
index to Bromley's
Travels, 45.
Register as a synonym of
index, 7, 8.
Remembrancia, Index to,
quoted, 85.
Repetition, Marks of, in
an index, 161, 204; in-
stances of incorrect use
of them, 80, 138.
Richardson (S.), index to
his three novels, 22.
—— a practised indexer, 22.

Royal Society attacked by
Dr. King, 42.
*Rules for Alphabetical
Indexes* (chap. vi.), 132-
171.
Rules for cataloguing re-
ferred to, 133.
Ruskin's *Fors Clavigera*,
Index to, 103.
Russell (Constance, Lady)
points out confusions in
indexes, 80.

"ST." to be arranged in the
alphabet as "Saint," 145.
Saints to be arranged under
their proper names, 145.
Scaliger, his index to
Gruter's *Thesaurus In-
scriptionum*, 88.
Schmidt (Dr. Alexander),
Shakespeare Lexicon
(1874), 120.
"Scholar's (A)" opposition
to publication of a subject-
index to the British
Museum library cata-
logue, 126.
Scientific books, Indexing
of, 120.
Scobell's *Acts and Or-
dinances of Parliament*,
the words "index" and
"table" both used, 9.
*Selwyn (George), and his
Contemporaries*, pub-
lished without an index,
84.
Seneca, his indication of the
contents of his books, 6.

Elliot Stock, Paternoster Row, London.

For EU product safety concerns, contact us at Calle de José Abascal, 56–1°, 28003 Madrid, Spain or eugpsr@cambridge.org.